PENNINE
WAY SOUTH

NATIONAL TRAIL GUIDES

PENNINE WAY
SOUTH

Tony Hopkins

Photographs by Simon Warner

AURUM PRESS

The
Countryside
Agency

ACKNOWLEDGEMENTS

For help with the 2002 revision, special thanks to Steve Westwood of the Countryside Agency. Also to Rick Hill, Steve Tipping, Don Askew, Peter Lambert and Mike Ogden.

This book is dedicated to the memory of Bill Fitchett, artist, naturalist and rambler.

Tony Hopkins is a freelance writer, illustrator and photographer with over 25 years' professional experience in conservation and countryside interpretation. He has worked at the British Museum, the Wildfowl and Wetlands Trust and at a Field Studies Centre, and was head of Visitor Services at Northumberland National Park. His other books include *The Cheviot Way of Life*, *Pennine Way North* and the Ordnance Survey Leisure Guide to the Peak District.

This revised edition first published 2003 by Aurum Press Ltd
in association with the Countryside Agency

A catalogue record for this book is available from the British Library.

ISBN 1 85410 851 4

Book design by Robert Updegraff
Cover photograph: *The Pennine Way at Hawes, N. Yorks*
(Simon Warner/Countryside Agency)
Title page photograph: *The extensive view westwards
from the summit of Fountains Fell.*

Printed and bound in Italy by Printer Trento Srl

CONTENTS

Circular walks appear on pages 58, 100, 102 and 122

HOW TO USE THIS GUIDE

The 268-mile (429-kilometre) Pennine Way is covered by two National Trail Guides. This book features the southern half of the Way, from Edale to Bowes (127 miles/204 kilometres). A companion guide features the Way from Bowes to Kirk Yetholm.

The guide is in three parts:

• The introduction, with an historical background to the trail and advice for walkers.

• The Pennine Way itself, split into ten chapters, with maps opposite the description for each route section. This part of the guide also includes information on places of interest and background features, as well as a number of circular walks which can be taken around each part of the Way. Key sites are numbered both in the text and on the maps to make it easier to follow the route description.

• The last part includes useful information, such as local transport, accommodation and organisations involved with the Pennine Way.

The maps have been prepared by the Ordnance Survey for this trail guide using 1:25 000 Explorer® or Outdoor Leisure® maps as a base. The line of the Pennine Way is shown in yellow, with the status, where known, of each section of the Way – footpath, bridleway or byway, for example – shown in green underneath (see key on inside front cover). In some cases, the yellow line on these maps may not coincide exactly with the right of way, or may show a route which is different from that shown in other guide books and maps. Walkers are recommended to follow the yellow route in this guide, which will eventually be the route that is waymarked with the distinctive acorn symbol ♣ used for all National Trails, or with cairns or posts on the higher stretches. In a few places the author has given alternative routes to follow; full details are in the text. Any parts of the Way that may be difficult to follow on the ground are clearly highlighted in the route description, and important points to watch for are marked with letters in each chapter, both in the text and on the maps. *Some maps start on a right-hand page and continue on the left-hand page – black arrows (➜) at the edge of the maps indicate the start point.*

In places the Pennine Way may be diverted from the line shown in this guide. Walkers are asked to follow the waymarks and observe any signs that indicate this.

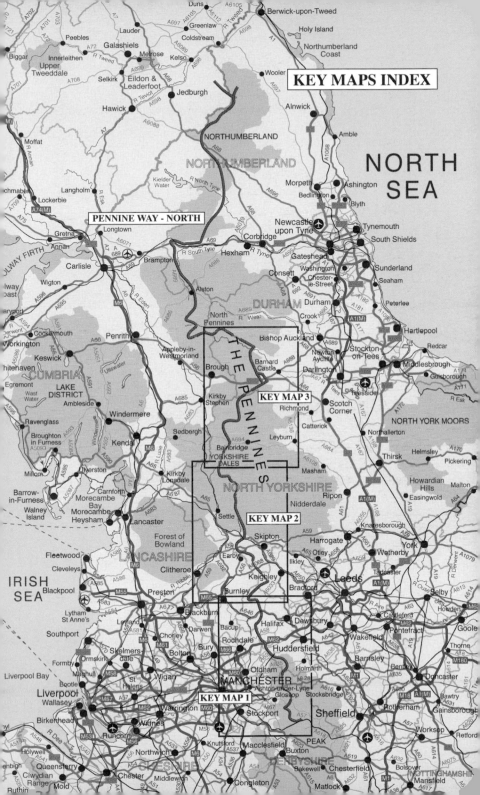

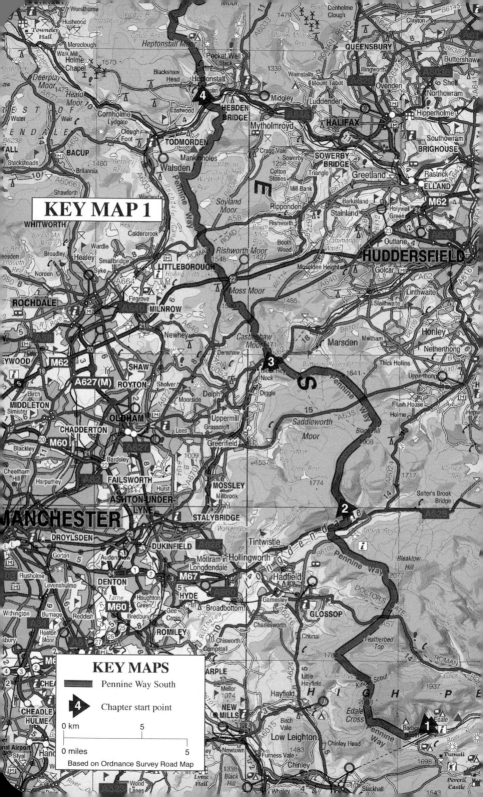

KEY MAP 1

KEY MAPS

━━━ Pennine Way South

◢**4** Chapter start point

0 km   5
0 miles   5

Based on Ordnance Survey Road Map

KEY MAP 2

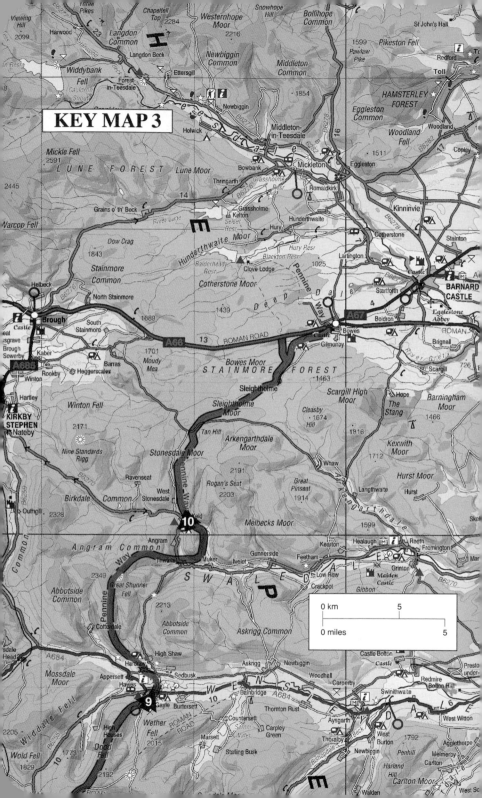

KEY MAP 3

Distance checklist

This list will assist you in calculating the distances between places on the southern part of the Pennine Way where you may be planning to stay overnight, or in checking your progress along the way.

location	approx. distance from previous location	
	miles	*km*
Edale	0	0
Kinder Downfall	4.9	7.9
A57 Snake Road	4.3	6.9
Bleaklow Head	2.3	3.7
Crowden	4.5	7.2
Black Hill	4.3	6.9
A635	1.7	2.7
Wessenden Reservoir	1.9	3.1
Standedge (A62)	3.1	5.0
M62 crossing	4.4	7.1
Warland Reservoir	4.9	7.9
Stoodley Pike	3.1	5.0
A646 (for Hebden Bridge)	2.4	3.9
Walshaw Dean Reservoirs	6.3	10.1
Ponden	4.4	7.1
Cowling	4.6	7.4
Lothersdale	2.5	4.0
Thornton-in-Craven	4.4	7.1
Gargrave	4.3	6.9
Malham	6.3	10.1
Malham Tarn	3.3	5.3
Pen-y-ghent	8.0	12.9
Horton in Ribblesdale	3.1	5.0
Cam Fell	6.4	10.3
Dodd Fell	3.0	4.8
Hawes	4.3	6.9
Great Shunner Fell	6.2	10.0
Thwaite	3.3	5.3
Keld	2.8	4.5
Tan Hill	4.0	6.4
Trough Heads	5.3	8.5
Bowes	3.2	5.1
[A66 (Pasture End) route avoiding Bowes]	1.2	1.9

PREFACE

The Pennine Way was Britain's first long-distance footpath, designated more than 30 years ago. This guide follows the southern section of the route, from Edale to Bowes, a distance of nearly 130 miles. Starting in the Peak District, it crosses the south Pennine moors before entering the unique landscape of the Yorkshire Dales National Park with its characteristic dry stone walls and field barns.

The peaty landscape of the Pennines has proved vulnerable to erosion by walkers but over the years the surface has been improved considerably by investment in restoration works. The nature of the terrain makes it very much a walkers' path, and in response to this the Countryside Agency is currently co-ordinating the development of the Pennine Bridleway, which will provide horse riders and cyclists with a similar trail through the Pennines that is suitable for their needs.

National Trails are promoted and defined by the Countryside Agency and maintained by local authorities. They are all waymarked with the distinctive acorn symbol which signals that you are on the right route.

I hope that you will enjoy this book in planning and undertaking your walk, and that it will enhance your pleasure on 'the backbone of Britain'.

Ewen Cameron
Chairman
Countryside Agency

PART ONE

INTRODUCTION

The origins of the Pennine Way

The Pennine Way was the first National Trail in Britain, officially opened on 24 April 1965, at a gathering of over 2,000 walkers at Malham Moor in the Yorkshire Dales. The project had gained ministerial approval in 1951 but it took a further 14 years for local authorities to open up the 70 miles (113 km) of new paths necessary to complete the route.

The original idea for a continuous Pennine walk appeared in a *Daily Herald* article in 1935, written by the rambler and journalist Tom Stephenson. He had been impressed by similar trails in the United States and had the vision to apply the concept of a wilderness path to the English Pennines. The country was ready and the suggestion was carried forward on the same heady wind of change that had demanded access to the hills and the establishment of National Parks. Most of the fieldwork for the Pennine Way was undertaken by the Ramblers' Association and the Youth Hostels Association in the late 1930s. The war only sharpened the nation's appetite for peace and the appreciation of its heritage, so the 1949 Act was carried through Parliament in a spirit of optimism.

Forty years later millions of people walk the countryside without considering their right to be there, which is as it should be. But there are still problems to be resolved. The Countryside Agency has renamed the original long-distance routes National Trails and established new routes. The Pennine Way stands as the first and most famous of high-hills walks; it is a demonstration of how people can find peace and freedom in an overcrowded age.

Maintaining the path

Over the years the Pennine Way has become a victim of its own success. Until recently there were serious erosion problems, particularly across Peak District moorland and on popular ridge walks through the Yorkshire Dales. However, a great deal of effort has now gone into repairing and improving the route; bridges and stiles have been installed, stone slabs and aggregate surfaces have replaced the worst peat-grooves. Although some traditionalists may lament the introduction of artificial surfaces, no one could ever enjoy wading through waterlogged peat.

Major repairs have brought major benefits to walkers, speeding up progress and allowing attention to stray to the landscape rather than be concentrated on placing one foot after another. Also, the repaired and resurfaced sections of the route are relatively few and far between and they settle down and weather so quickly that they are soon indistinguishable from old packhorse trails. To help the ground to recover, some parts of the Way have been diverted on to paths better able to withstand the pressure. In other places, walkers have taken unofficial short cuts – some recommended in other guide books. Where these offer a better alternative, the route may be amended, and signed accordingly. Things are still changing and there may be places where official waymarks and stiles clearly indicate a route that differs from the map, in which case you should always be guided by the markers on the ground.

The southern half of the Pennine Way begins at the Nags Head in Edale, at the heart of the Peak District National Park.

Bleak mid-winter: Haworth Moor looking towards Top Withins.

How to walk the Way

Some people complete the Pennine Way in ten days and complain afterwards that it was nothing more than an endurance test. Others take a month and return home refreshed and happy. Personal achievement is impossible to measure against time and distance. This book sets out to guide walkers along the southern half of the Pennine Way, from Edale in Derbyshire to Bowes in County Durham. It does this in ten sections; a companion volume deals with the northern half of the Way in nine sections, thus implying that the whole Trail should take 19 days. This is a reasonable estimate based on a sensible itinerary, but there are many alternatives. One of the pleasures of a long walk is in planning it to suit yourself. There is no obligation to start from Edale, or to do the entire distance in one go. Some natural units, such as the crossing of the Dales, make ideal weekend projects and many day-length walks offer unrivalled opportunities to see high country. It is possible to build the whole Trail slowly by taking it in sections, separated by weeks, months or years, or to select the most dramatic stretches and pack them into a few unforgettable days. The nature of the Pennines makes it difficult to find circular routes which give a true impression of the landscape, but a few are included in the book which incorporate parts of the Way and stand on their own as good walks. Of course, nothing will quite compare with the sense of achievement, of weary exhilaration, that comes from completing the whole route as it was intended.

Landscape along the Way

The southern half of the Pennine Way begins at the Nag's Head in Edale, in the heart of the Peak National Park. From here the old route climbed Grindsbrook and crossed the Kinder plateau, but the present version of the Way follows a clearer and better route to Kinder Downfall via Jacob's Ladder.

North of the Downfall you pick your way over the bare moors of Mill Hill, Moss Castle and Featherbed Moss before crossing the Snake Road and climbing to Bleaklow. This can be a treacherous place and is an early test of resolve, but it can also be inspiring and the path is well maintained. Then you descend to Crowden, by Torside Reservoir in Longdendale, before the climb via Laddow Rocks to Black Hill. This is another place of evil repute, but most of the stories are travellers' tales and the descent via Wessenden Reservoir is more straightforward than it used to be. From Standedge the Way crosses gritstone moorland, over the M62 and past a series of reservoirs to Stoodley Pike and into Calderdale, a cradle of the Industrial Revolution. North of Hebden Bridge there are fields and pastures before more reservoirs and moorland around the Brontë country of Withins, Ponden and Haworth. Another block of moorland lies between Ponden and Ickornshaw, after which the route becomes a pastoral ramble through Gargrave to Airton and Malham in the Yorkshire Dales National Park.

Malham marks the beginning of a unique karst landscape, from the famous cove to the tarn and north to Pen-y-ghent and Horton in Ribblesdale. From here the Way climbs gradually to the open fells and follows a Roman road and packhorse trail over Cam Fell to Hawes in Wensleydale, then to Great Shunner Fell and so to the beautiful meadowland of Swaledale and the village of Keld. Then it continues north across Stonesdale Moor to Tan Hill on the National Park's northern boundary. All that remains is Stainmore, and the route now heads north-east over boggy Sleightholme Moor to the A66, and continues to the northern half of the Way (described in National Trail Guide no. 6), or along the 'Bowes Loop' into the little town of Bowes – the halfway point.

Planning your walk

The Pennine Way can be dangerous, so preparation is important. If you have never tried hill walking, test yourself over a few days or weekends in the Lake District or Brecon Beacons before deciding to take on the Pennine Way. Many young people find they are naturally fit but lack stamina; older people still have the potential for excellent stamina but lack basic strength. It is never too late to get fit, but the older you are, the more gentle should be the programme. Some kind of exercise which makes you sweaty and breathless for 20 minutes every two or three days is an ideal level of preparation, to be built up gradually. If you can cope with this, a day or two on the Pennine Way should hold no fears at all. However, to cope with the whole walk, day after day, requires extra stamina which can only be earned the hard way, on the hills.

To avoid blisters or sore feet, boots should be thoroughly worn in and socks absorbent, and without lumpy seams. Hardening the skin on the soles and heels helps, by applying alcohol or surgical spirit for a few weeks before a big walk. If blisters form, prick them and apply a porous plaster to keep the dead skin in place over the tender new layer underneath. Keep your toe nails clipped and make sure your boots fit properly.

Your first-aid kit should contain plasters, pain-relief tablets, something to treat diarrhoea, something to treat midge bites (hydrocortisone cream rather than antihistamine, which can cause a reaction) and insect repellent (e.g. oil of citronella or deet). Lip salve can help wind-dried lips and Vaseline can help to soothe sore or chapped skin. It is best to know a little about first aid, and to be aware of the treatment for gastroenteritis (drink clear fluids with glucose and a little salt), exposure (glucose, warm dry clothing and a quick walk to shelter) and adder bites (seldom fatal but should not be ignored – immobilise the affected area and seek medical advice).

Essential clothing for a day on the Pennines should include a set of waterproofs (cagoule, overtrousers), a pair of warm trousers and a pullover. You may not need any of these items, but they should be packed in the rucksack just in case. There is no need to invest in heavyweight mountain boots. Lighter walking boots with ankle support, to reduce the risk of sprained ankles, and a degree of waterproofing, are more than adequate and much better than trainers even on dry ground. Fully enclosed gaiters and strong mountain boots will keep your feet dry even after crossing Kinder or the Cheviot. A good rucksack deserves as much loyalty as a comfortable pair of boots. Some are top-heavy, some have narrow or slipping straps and some absorb rainwater like a sponge. Some do all these and still cost a great deal of money. Into the (waterproof) rucksack should go a compass and a set of appropriate maps, so don't forget this book!

Food and an adequate supply of drink (probably more than you think) and money (ditto) complete the basic list, to which can be added camera, notebook and whatever else you feel inclined to take with you. Company, or the deliberate avoidance of it, will of course be the nub of one of the most important decisions before the start of the walk. Safety, making sure someone knows where you are, is even more important for lone walkers than it is for groups. Anyone undertaking the whole walk will also need to think carefully about accommodation, whether they are youth hostelling, bed and breakfasting or camping, for this will affect how much they carry and where they need to pick up provisions. Useful information, including a list of addresses, appears on pages 138–44.

Looking back along the walled track that comes down from Pen-y-ghent to Horton in Ribblesdale.

PART TWO

PENNINE WAY SOUTH
Edale to Bowes

1 Edale to Crowden

via Kinder Downfall and Bleaklow
16 miles (25.7 km)

The first few steps of the Pennine Way are generally reckoned to be from the threshold of the Old Nag's Head at Edale **1**, where you share the route with holidaymakers sauntering up and down the narrow road that links the five Booth villages.

Unless you have made arrangements to be picked up on the A57 Snake Road, the first day will be a testing 16 miles (26 km), climbing from green pastures to the bleak gritstone moors of Kinder, from the mires of Featherbed Moss across deep peat clefts or groughs, and up to the stony wilderness of Bleaklow. Then the Way will take you on to Torside Reservoir and Crowden in Longdendale.

On a fine day the Dark Peak, as this part of Derbyshire is called, can be food for the soul, but on a day of leaden mist and cloying peat it can starve any walker's resolve. Most people who fail to complete the Pennine Way give up after the first or second day, unaware that their stamina and confidence – and perhaps also the landscape – get better and better as they head north.

From Edale, the old route of the Way heads north-west following Grinds Brook up and over Kinder Scout. This can still be followed, but by taking what was once described as a bad-weather alternative, to the west of the Kinder plateau, you follow a much better and more interesting path. This is now the recommended route of the Pennine Way and avoids extremely eroded stretches.

Take the path signed 'Pennine Way' to the left of a track on the opposite side of the road from the Old Nag's Head, in the shadow of a tall walnut tree. From here, follow the sunken path called Peat Lane, adjacent to a stream. The hedges are of hawthorn, with ash and holly: trees and shrubs of the managed countryside. These soon give way to rowan and birch, more typical of the uplands.

From Peat Lane turn left over a stile and into a pasture, following a path parallel with the slopes of Broadlee-Bank Tor. The view of the surrounding peaks is excellent; to the north-east is Ringing Roger and Nether Tor, and across the green valley of the River Noe, directly south, is Rushup Edge and Mam Tor. Mam Tor, sometimes known as the Shivering Mountain because of its impressive face of fragile, silvery shale, marks the start of the Dark Peak; beyond lies beautiful limestone country, the White Peak of the Derbyshire Dales. Much of this area was once part of the Royal Forest of the Peak, a hunting preserve created for William the Conqueror as a chase and given to his son William Peveril. It was then partly wooded with oak and birch; in later years, relaxation of the forest laws saw a gradual expansion of heathland, and the remnants of the forest were enclosed as a deer park in Elizabethan times.

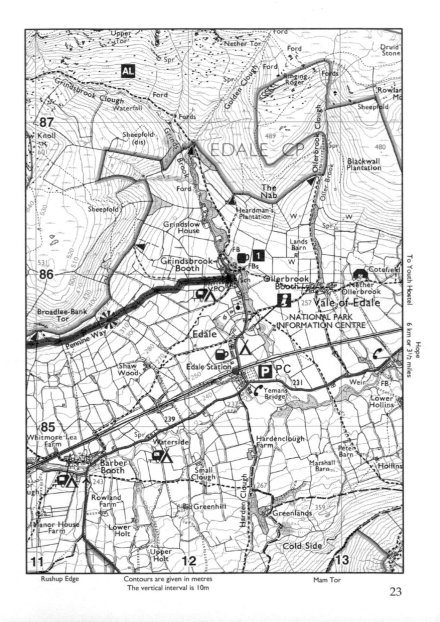

Rushup Edge   Contours are given in metres   Mam Tor
                   The vertical interval is 10m

Continue to a post on a grassy rise, then bear left of the post (that is, straight on in the direction marked Pennine Way via Jacobs Ladder, not to the right in the direction marked Crowden Brook) and so downhill, south-west to meet a muddy track leading through Upper Booth Farm **2**, owned by the National Trust. Turn right along a metalled road, crossing Crowden Brook in the shade of some fine sessile oak, wych-elm, alder, rowan and sycamore.

Through a gate, the track leads to Lee Farm, past a little information shelter **3** for the National Trust's High Peak Estate, and north-west to a packhorse bridge. Beyond this lies unenclosed moorland, with the rocky outcrops of the Wool Packs and Crowden Tower visible on the skyline to the north. This track used to be an important cross-Pennine route carrying salt to Yorkshire and wool back to Cheshire. Once across the little bridge, the ponies going westwards followed a zigzag track up the hillside. One of the 'jaggers' or herders is reputed to have

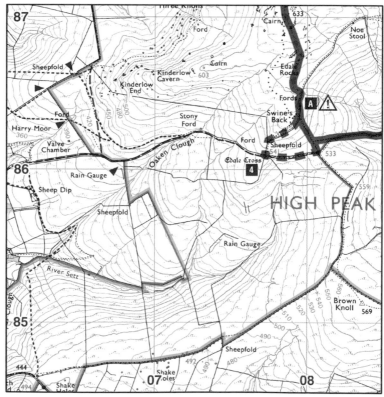

Contours are given in metres
The vertical interval is 10m

taken a quick short cut up the steepest slope so that he could have enough time to smoke a pipe before his train of horses arrived – hence the name Jacob's Ladder.

After the sharp ascent of a grassy slope with gorse, bracken and stunted rowans, climbing a well-maintained set of rocky steps, the Way leads, still quite steeply, to a gate. At this point turn right through the heather to continue or take an optional detour along the track to see Edale Cross **4** – signed as a medieval cross, but in fact a boundary marker for the Royal Forest of the Peak, which once stood in romantic isolation but has now been enclosed on three sides by a tall dry stone wall. From just east of the cross, turn north beside a wall, bearing north-east to rejoin the main route at a gap in the wall. From here continue north for a little way beside the wall, then turn uphill to a rocky area. Bear left along a stone-surfaced path to the large cairn **A** (take care not to miss this). At the cairn bear left to an outcrop of gritstone called Edale Rocks.

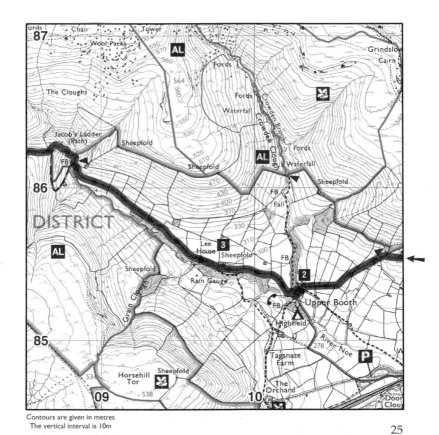

Contours are given in metres
The vertical interval is 10m

Pass to the east of these rocks, then the Way continues north-north-west along an indistinct path across a lunar terrain of gritty pebbles and bare, black peat. Intermittent cairns mark the route. There are encouraging signs of heather regeneration following a management policy by the National Trust – take sheep off the land and apply lime to stimulate plant growth. To ascend to Kinder Low keep to the left (west) of the triangulation point (spot height 2,076 feet/633 metres) then bear north-north-east along the stony edge above Kinder Reservoir.

In poor visibility this path is still easy to follow, crossing Red Brook and continuing past occasional cairns towards Kinder Downfall **5**. Occasionally mountain hares appear among the boulders (the species was introduced into the area over a century ago) and curlew and golden plovers fly overhead. Kinder Downfall **5**, a little waterfall that sometimes becomes a torrent, lies in a rocky chasm out of all proportion to its present status. While transporting glacial meltwater it must have been a chaotic and impressive sight but now, waiting for the next ice age, it is a tamed spirit.

After rock-hopping just above the Downfall, you head north-west, still on the rocky edge above Kinder Reservoir, with an attractive block of woodland visible beyond the reservoir on the west bank of the River Kinder and, on a clear day, Manchester in the distance. The rock-forms along the edge are attractive, the precursors of many caps of Millstone Grit on South Pennine ridges, weathered into impressive shapes. The vegetation is sparse once again, with some intermittent crowberry and bilberry, but also a great deal of bare peat.

Cross a fence and old wall **B**. Continuing along the rocky edge you eventually reach a cairn, then there is a sharp descent to a gravel path over a marshy saddle. Ignore the stone-slabbed path to the left. As you begin to climb again you cross a well-worn footpath. Close to this crossroad is a Stone Age 'flint factory' **6** – a place where flints were knapped for use as spear or arrow points, or for scrapers to prepare skins.

From the cairn on top of Mill Hill the route is clear as it turns to the north-east (right) as a stone-slabbed path on the top of a broad crest, usually flushed pink by the leaves of cotton-grass. The Way now heads towards Moss Castle, with a good view to the right of Fair-brook Naze on the northern edge of the Kinder plateau. The route bears in a more easterly direction as you approach Glead Hill, then once again resumes its north-easterly course **C** towards Featherbed Moss. The word 'glead' or 'gled'

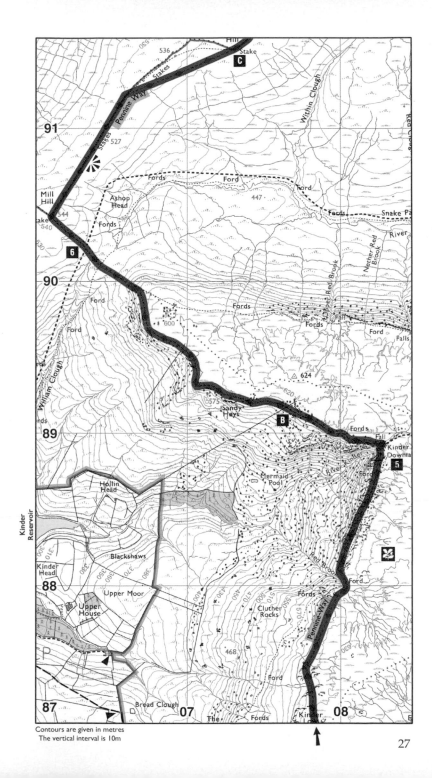

Contours are given in metres
The vertical interval is 10m

27

Looking across the fields from Grinsbrook towards Upper Booth.

refers to a bird of prey. Although it was usually applied to the red kite – a woodland bird – it seems more likely that it was used here to describe hen or Montagu's harriers, which probably nested on these moors in medieval times.

In good visibility the A57 Snake Road (between Glossop and Sheffield) will by now be a tempting sight but it is important to keep to the path, partly because of hidden bogs and partly because the land is a private grouse moor (hence no harriers these days). Featherbed Moss marks what used to be the most notorious and difficult section of the Pennine Way to navigate. It has now been tamed by a stone-slabbed path, making progress altogether quicker and more comfortable. The only possible danger lies in short cuts, which should be resisted. The word 'featherbed' seems wholly inappropriate, but is an ironic reference to the sheets of cotton-grass – beautiful, soft and white, idly tossed over a sodden black mattress.

Snake Road is crossed almost directly and the route to the north is level and firm. After crossing a stile and continuing north-east, you arrive at the Doctor's Gate **7**, an east–west cleft marked on maps as a Roman road, although most of the visible remains, including sandstone slabs and kerbs, are of medieval origin. In the 16th century, a doctor from Glossop with a wide circle of friends and patients is reputed to have adopted the byway.

The ghosts of Romans and robbers seem very close on the lonely approach to Bleaklow. Clammy mists pervade the place more often than not. After crossing the Doctor's Gate **7** you follow the Devil's Dike, a deep, wide furrow or 'grough' in the peat. The going is better along the bottom of the grough

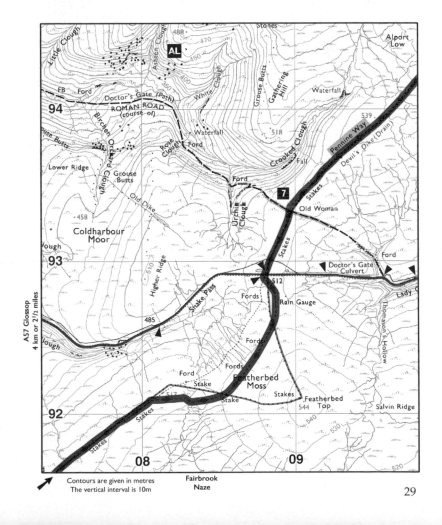

Contours are given in metres
The vertical interval is 10m

Fairbrook
Naze

than on its shoulder, even when conditions are very wet. A legend concerning the Devil's Dike tells of an alchemist (or 'Doctor') who once sold his soul to the Devil and tried to win it back in a horse race along Doctor's Gate. By leaping the Dike just ahead of the Devil, the doctor managed to put water between them and so break the spell. The true history of the Dike is obscure – it may mark a Saxon boundary. Eventually, after heading north-east along the ditch for some distance, you meet a short stretch of stone-slabbed path, then follow a dry channel. The route is waymarked **D**. Now head north-west to meet Hern Clough, and follow the stony stream as it winds to the left.

The bilberry hereabouts grows in large tussocks. A few birds find the vast loneliness irresistible; there are usually pipits and grouse, and this is one of the few places in the country where dunlin (common visitors to the British coast but rare breeders) are likely to be seen.

Hern Clough narrows and eventually disappears; you continue north along a waymarked stream channel, as far as Bleaklow Head. The path has stone-slabbed sections and follows a clear route; but if in doubt, look for footprints ahead. Away to the left are the Herne Stones **8**, and you can make a short detour to take a closer look. Stories of Herne the hunter, a spectral hunter said to haunt Windsor Forest, come to mind. From Bleaklow Head it is also possible to take a detour to the Wain Stones **9**, another collection of heavily weathered gritstone boulders, two of which, when viewed from the right angle, have Neanderthal profiles and appear to be kissing.

Head north following the waymarks. This leads to a huge cairn. The terrain on the broad dome of Bleaklow summit (2,076 feet/633 metres) is quite different from the approach, as is often the case. The surface of the ground is like a sandy desert, paved here and there by gritstone boulders. Black mounds or pyramids show how the covering of peat has been reduced and dispersed by the winds. The pale dust of the post-glacial uplands, now leached of its minerals, lies at your feet.

Head north **E**, following the stone posts, then north-west and finally westwards, down a cleft that gradually becomes clearly defined as a small stream (or 'grain'). The route keeps to the northern side of Wildboar Grain until it drops down to the confluence of the streams at John Track Well **F**. Crossing the clough turn north-west to follow a steep-sided valley. At last views open out. A clear paved path maintains the height of the

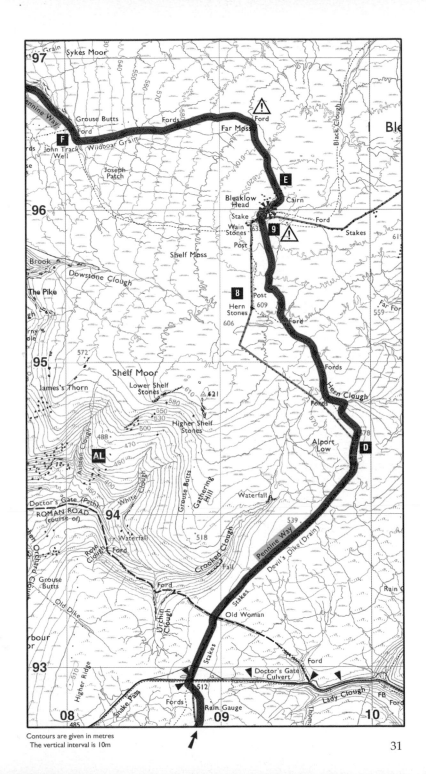

Contours are given in metres
The vertical interval is 10m

31

The descent from Bleaklow Head into Longdendale.

route as the valley becomes deeper. This is Torside Clough. Heather becomes more luxuriant, rock pillars and boulders frame fine views to Torside Reservoir. Everything suddenly seems less threatening. Eventually the path descends steeply to a track; turn left here down to a road. Cross over and turn right (signed Trans-Pennine Trail and Pennine Way), then turn left after a picnic spot **G**. You then cross the dam wall between

Rhodeswood and Torside Reservoirs and, just after the spillway bridge, turn right **H** up a flight of stone steps.

At a white stile turn right and walk through the pine plantation and then up to the road, the A628(T), and obliquely right, heading east and north-east up a stony track. This is a new, improved route. Just beyond another plantation you arrive at a junction **I**. If you intend to stop at Crowden, continue down to cross the Crowden Brook, close to the camp site and youth hostel. If you wish to continue walking, the Pennine Way is signposted to the left.

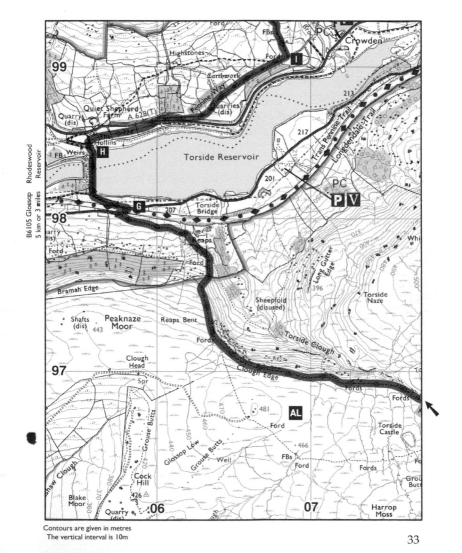

Contours are given in metres
The vertical interval is 10m

2 Crowden to Standedge

over Black Hill and across Wessenden Moor
11 miles (17.7 km)

From Crowden to Standedge, the second section of the Pennine Way reaches the northern boundary of the Peak National Park, continuing through brooding moorland. There is a long ascent over Laddow Rocks to Black Hill. People who have walked the whole route from Edale may now be suffering from fatigue but in general this is an easier and shorter day.

Longdendale has suffered over the centuries from being a convenient corridor for east–west access and communications. From the Middle Ages it was used as a packhorse route for salt, minimising possible tolls by allowing the traders and jaggers to follow the Cheshire panhandle and cross directly into Yorkshire. This was superseded by a turnpike route in 1731, and during the Industrial Revolution the River Etherow, one of the three main tributaries of the Mersey, provided water power for a series of mills and factories. The famous Woodhead railway tunnel above Woodhead Reservoir was built between 1838 and 1845. Twenty-eight people were killed in a cholera outbreak during the construction of a second railway tunnel; most of them were buried in the little church of St James. The reservoirs that now dominate Longdendale were created in the 1870s. They, like the road and even the great pylons, now look as if they belong here, although the wilderness is never far away.

From Crowden the Pennine Way becomes a dry stony track high above the west bank of Crowden Brook. To the right, the mixed plantation (birch, rowan, oak, larch, pine) sometimes acts as a stopover for migrating birds. Past the plantation, you head north-north-west towards the impressive face of Laddow Rocks. The view back across the dale allows a farewell glimpse of the tableland of Bleaklow, scarred by Wildboar Clough. White drifts of mat grass contrast with the black heather of the upper slopes. The route heads obliquely uphill below Black Tor and Rakes Rocks among boulders, steepening to cross Oaken-clough Brook **A**. When you reach the top of the sandstone ridge to follow the cliff top, there is an excellent view of the main face of Laddow Rocks **10**, popular among Manchester climbers since the 'discovery' of the Pennines at the turn of the century. It was first explored by E. A. Baker and others in 1901, and in 1916 the Norwegian, Ivar Berg, bivouacked in the cave and climbed Cave Crack and Cave Arête wearing clogs.

Looking back across Longdendale it is easy to picture late-glacial Britain by imagining the chaos caused by retreating ice. Moraines, landslips and soil-creep were the result of climatic changes over 10,000 years ago, yet their effects are clearly visible on the broadening valley floor of the Crowden Brook. Above the ribs of sandstone it is also possible to imagine the process of peat formation that blackened Bareholme Moss **11** and transformed it from fertile woodland into a distinctly barren mire.

The Way continues along the top of the crags, close to the edge, with some fine rock-forms visible below. A path to the left **B**, marked by a cairn on the top of Laddow Rocks at 1,650 feet (502 metres), leads to Chew Reservoir (the highest in the country) on the eastern outskirts of Manchester. The Way itself continues north-north-east to cross some marshy ground, where nutrient flushes have allowed plants such as marsh thistle and

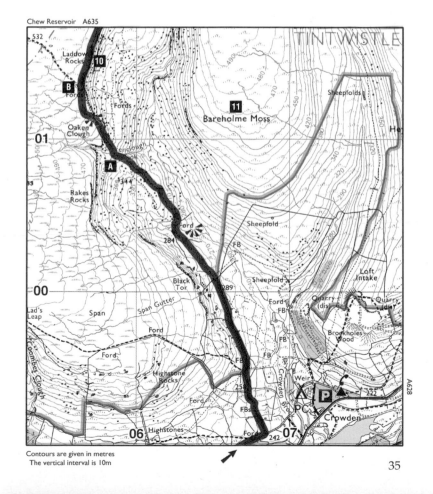

Contours are given in metres
The vertical interval is 10m

bog violet to find a place in what is now an austere landscape. The route crosses side streams draining Black Chew Head and Near and Far Broadslate; these are usually easily forded, but as the gradient increases towards Black Hill the whole hillside becomes waterlogged and you begin to rely again on stone slabs. Most of the slopes are covered with cotton-grass. During the autumn the leaves turn a beautiful orange and in early summer the fluffy white flowers are pretty. Common cotton-grass has loose, drooping flowerheads of long, silky hairs, usually two or three heads on each stem. On drier ground (not very noticeable just here) look for hare's-tail common grass; it has single, more compact flowers. Get to know your cotton-grasses and you may manage to steer clear of the worst bogs.

Black Hill **12** once had a nightmare reputation: literally, the black spot of the whole Pennine Way. Anyone who ever had reservations about the desirability of stone slabs (or sets) along the route has only to take a brisk stroll over Black Hill to be convinced. Where once there was doom and despondency, there is now cheery enthusiasm. The route follows Crowden Great Brook until its confluence with Meadowgrain Clough **C**, after which there is a straight ascent north-east over Dun Hill to the broad summit on the Derbyshire/Yorkshire border. At 1,910 feet (582 metres), Black Hill used to be the highest point in Cheshire, but even this modest claim to fame has passed into history. A sea of wind-blown peat surrounds a triangulation column in the middle of the level hilltop; this black blanket stretches for over 220 yards (200 metres) and used to make the column virtually unattainable. More than one reckless adventurer has had to be rescued after getting stuck fast while trying to pose for a photograph here. Walking along the slabbed path today is like tiptoeing past caged lions: you know you are safe but there is still an adrenalin rush from being so close to danger.

On most maps the point where the column stands is called Soldiers' Lump, to commemorate the efforts of the Royal Engineers who surveyed the place in the 19th century. From the summit of Black Hill, the Pennine Way used to head north-west, over Dean Head Moss and Featherbed Moss – names that give a clue to the prevailing conditions underfoot. However, a major alteration now carries the route over much better terrain, heading north-north-east. This whole landscape has affinities with Arctic Norway – a place of low cloud, bitter winds, peat flows and exposed gravels. Tundra flowers eke out a precarious existence, waiting for the next ice age.

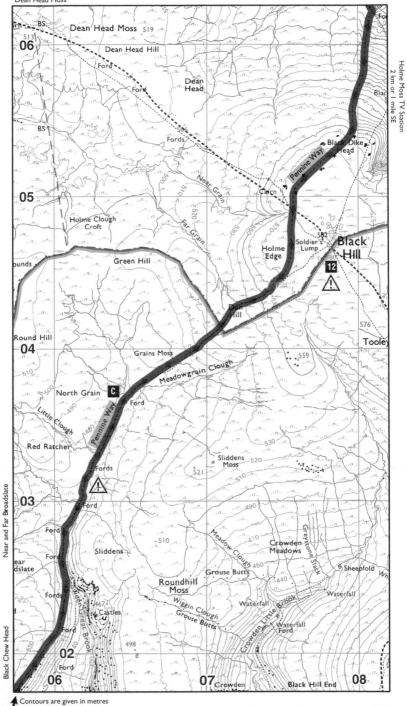

Featherbed Moss
Dean Head Moss

Dean Head Moss 519
Dean Head Hill
Ford
Dean Head
Ford

06

BS

BS

Fords

05

Holme Clough Croft

Green Hill

Near Grain

Far Grain

Cairn

Pennine Way

Black Dike Head

Holme Edge

Soldier's Lump

Black Hill

582
580

12

⚠

Holme Moss TV Station
2 km or 1 mile SE

Blac

For

Bush Hill

Round Hill

04

Grains Moss

Meadowgrain Clough

559

576

Tooley

North Grain

C

Ford

Pennine Way

Little Clough

Red Ratcher

Fords

⚠

530

Sliddens Moss 520

521

510

Greystone Slack

Sheepfold

Waterfall

03

Ford

Ford

Ford

Fords

Fords

Sliddens

510

Meadow Clough

470

450

Crowden Meadows

440

Grouse Butts

Waterfall

Near and Far Broadslate

Black Chew Head

Roundhill Moss

Wiggin Clough
Grouse Butts

Castles

467

02

Ford

498

06

07

Crowden Little Brook

Waterfall Ford

Wh

Crowden

Black Hill End

08

⬆ Contours are given in metres
The vertical interval is 10m

37

Cotton-grass and peaty pools on Black Hill summit.

Mountain hares are common hereabouts among the cotton-grass near the summit, and can sometimes be seen in their white winter coats as late as June. They are smaller than common hares and have shorter ears. Although they occur over most of Scotland, this is the only area in England where you are likely to see them. Foxes also find their way on to the moors, particularly during the summer months when they enjoy sitting out among the heather. Pennine foxes are reputed to be bigger than those of the south and east, despite their sparser diet.

As you leave the plateau a view opens out ahead. Prominent in the distance is the large wind generator at Longley Farm near Holmfirth. Nearer at hand is the slender 750-foot TV mast at Holme Moss, seemingly balanced like a pencil point. The pivot at its base allows it to sway in a gale, and when it was built in 1951 it was the world's most powerful transmitter. The mast is a useful landmark (except in thick mist!), as it marks the nearest road to Black Hill, and a means of escape in any emergency.

Tumbling cascades of whisky-coloured water are never far from the path.

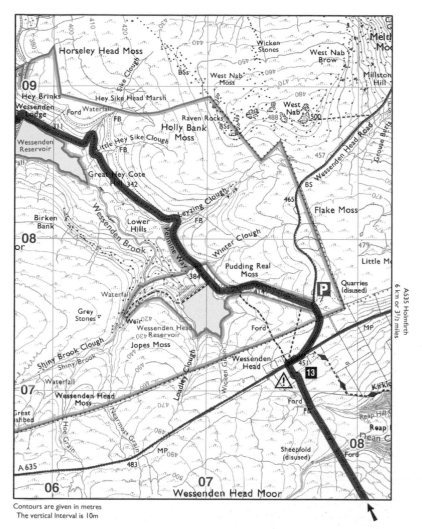

Contours are given in metres
The vertical Interval is 10m

A path across the shoulder above Issue Clough cuts the corner here and leads steeply downhill to a boundary ditch, which, together with the stone-slabbed path, forms a straight landmark heading directly towards the A635 road.

The Way crosses the road at the site of the Isle of Skye Inn **13** (one of the famous 'Four Inns' of the challenge walk), which was demolished in the 1950s for fear of polluting the nearby reservoirs. Turn right and walk for a short distance on the A635, then bear left along a side road for about 300 yards/metres towards Malham, and take the track on the left leading down to Wessenden Brook.

41

Wessenden Beck, an attractive little stream draining Saddleworth Moor.

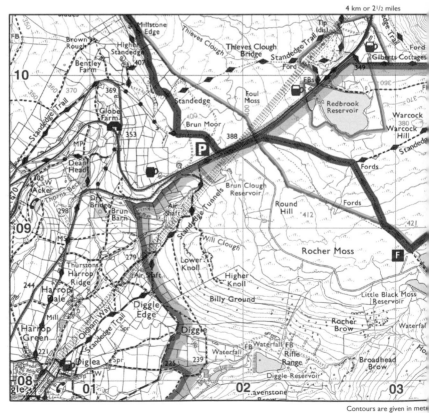

The official Pennine Way route continues past Wessenden Reservoir before heading north-west. Turn sharp left downhill to cross a stream **D**, then west along Blakely Clough. However, many walkers still use the old route: across the dam of the reservoir on to a good path that contours the hillside along a conduit to cross a stream at a weir below a waterfall, then climbs up out of the Wessenden Valley at Blakely Clough. The bare bones of the landscape protrude all along these deep cloughs, whose steep sides boast some impressive gritstone outcrops.

At the top of the slope **E**, bear right on a path which leads to the embankment of Black Moss Reservoir. Follow this path, keeping to the top of the bank. Continue to follow the path and then soon turn sharp right at a junction with a sandy track **F** just beyond Black Moss Reservoir, in line with the dam. Following the line of the stone-slabbed path, bear right, to descend to the old turnpike road, then turn left along the road which leads to the A62 Manchester to Huddersfield road at Standedge Cutting.

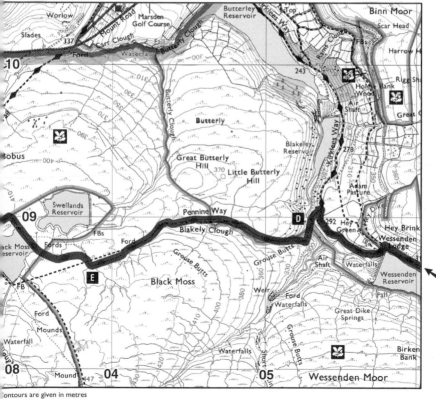

Contours are given in metres
The vertical interval is 10m

Peat

Peat formation began a very long time ago. Until 7,500 years ago the British climate was cool and dry, after the long tundra phase that followed the Ice Age. Open woodland of pine and birch covered the uplands, and the surface of the ground would have been firm and grassy. Then, for about 2,000 years, a mild damp atmosphere hung over western Europe, and plants grew in profusion. Oak, elm, small-leaved lime and ash spread up the valleys and on to the plateaux. Hazel was common in the Peak District, and must have lined most of the cloughs.

The amount of rain began to affect the rich soils. Minerals were washed downwards and the surface became water-logged, making it impossible for bacteria to rot away the vegetation. Gradually, a top layer of black, undecayed plant debris accumulated, at about an inch (2.5 cm) a century. The activities of Neolithic settlers, in clearing the tree cover and exposing the ground to even more rain, must have accelerated the process. Eventually, the higher ground had open spaces covered by *Sphagnum* moss. By the time the climate turned drier, the process was unstoppable.

For the past 5,000 years the Peak moors have been carpeted in peat to an average depth of $3^1/_4$ feet (1 metre). Waterlogged mires, fed by rain rather than groundwater, are very acidic and poor in nutrients, so few plants are able to thrive. *Sphagnum* (bog) moss is the most important, and for centuries it was the major ingredient in succeeding layers of peat. Plant fragments preserved in peat make it possible to identify leaves and pollen grains that are thousands of years old, and so build up a picture of what the countryside once looked like. In many places, such as Bleaklow and Black Hill, parts of the peat cover have been worn away to leave 'hags', steep-faced islands where the whole history of post-glacial Britain is visible as a multi-layered profile. The thin surface layer of peat is much blacker than the rest, due to atmospheric pollution over the past 200 years, and there has been a sharp decline in the amount of *Sphagnum* and a corresponding increase in cotton-grass, which now dominates the South Pennine 'mosses'.

The interlocking surface growth of *Sphagnum*, and its capacity to absorb water, means that a crust of vegetation on a wet moor is easily broken, creating flows which are soon turned into deep channels or 'groughs'. It takes only a few walkers to turn a moss into a morass.

Blanket bog is a rare habitat worldwide. Moss and sedge communities are easily damaged; it's not only walkers who benefit from stone-slabbed paths.

3 Standedge to Hebden Bridge

over the M62 and via Stoodley Pike
15 miles (24.1 km)

Standedge cutting is little more than a groove accommodating the high-speed traffic on the A62. Manchester lies to the south-west, Huddersfield to the north-east.

The most interesting feature lies several hundred feet beneath your feet; railway and canal tunnels run for 3 miles (5 km) through the sandstone bedrock between the village of Diggle in Greater Manchester and Marsden in West Yorkshire. The Huddersfield Narrow Canal tunnel, the longest in the country, has recently been re-opened, and there is a visitor center at Standedge.

From Standedge this section of the Way keeps to the high moors and gritstone edges, and its points of reference are the arterial roads and impounded reservoirs serving the great conurbations on each side of the Pennine ridge. Years of air pollution have blackened the rock, killing any colourful lichens that might have added a dab of colour. The sheep have sooty fleeces. From the car park **A** north of the little Brun Clough Reservoir the route crosses the A62. You make your way up a sandy track, then bear left for 100 yards to a track junction. The Way turns right a further 100 yards beyond here, by a small quarry, with views to the left across Globe Farm and the main road towards Diggle. You continue along a well-worn path and head up to the Standedge ridge, before heading north-west towards the triangulation point **B** atop Millstone Edge.

The edges, shallow cliffs of millstone grit, look over one of the most densely populated landscapes in Europe. The huge slabs and boulders are weathered into some outlandish shapes, good for photography. Past the triangulation point **B** (at 1,470 feet/448 metres) the route keeps to the lip of the gritstone, making the contrast even more stark; to the west are valleys and farms, and little reservoirs with clumps of lollipop pines. Ahead lies the wilderness, created through centuries of farming but nevertheless a wild and lonely place.

Just after the Millstone Edge triangulation point **B** you pass the Ammon Wrigley Memorial Stone (dedicated to a Saddleworth writer of local fame) and the Dinner Stone, then along the edge and across several shallow cloughs before turning northeast to make for the hill crest. The terrain so far is typical of

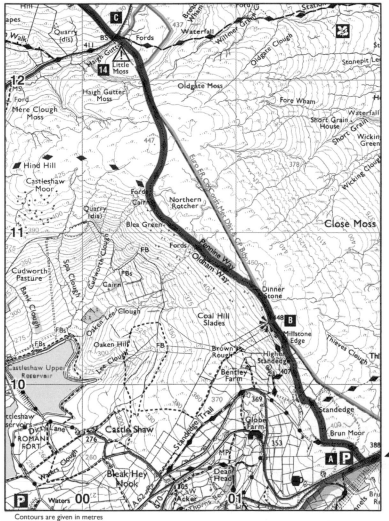

Contours are given in metres
The contour values are 5m and 10m

degraded moorland, with slopes of bare peat and sand and patches of bent-grass and cotton-grass. At first the path is stony and dry, but when the route turns away from the gritstone edge above Blea Green, and after a more obvious stream head, you have to traverse a dome of sodden peat, where path reconstruction work has taken place to minimise erosion. You go north then north-west by Oldgate Moss to the smaller dome of Little Moss **14**. After this there is a descent to meet the A640 (Huddersfield–Denshaw) road at an old packhorse trail **C**, which leads obliquely eastwards. This used to be a tricky part of the route, but the path is now surfaced with aggregate and the crossing place is usually dry.

The A640 was one of the turnpike roads established during the 18th century and run as a profit-making venture by Turnpike Trusts until the coming of the railways in the mid-19th century. Most of the revenue came from carriages and carts; cross-Pennine commerce was in full swing and a toll of 6d (2.5p) per draught animal brought a healthy return to the trustees or investors. Canals carried much of the raw material, at one-third of the cost, but were much slower.

After crossing the road **C** you head north-west, uphill, making for what looks like a rock outcrop or cairn on the skyline, although it is in fact the end of a wall **D**. You continue beside the wall, with the brow of Rape Hill away to the left, then drop down to cross a shallow clough **E** (with a view of Readycon Dean Reservoir to the left), before rising again to the brow of White Hill. Underfoot is now an aggregate path, but it is easy to appreciate how difficult the going used to be before improvements were made to the Way: black peat alternates with white sand or gravel to either side and the ground is either waterlogged or bone dry.

Soon after White Hill the Way veers north-north-west **F**, below the northern slopes of Green Hole Hill, then descends along Axletree Edge with the radio mast of Windy Hill and the M62 directly ahead. Another old turnpike road is negotiated before these more dominant recent features; this is the A672, crossed at a lay-by **G**. A weathered old stone sign marks the county boundary, where West Yorkshire and Calderdale are entered. The lay-by often boasts a tea-van selling hot snacks to travellers. Otherwise head northwards, passing to the right of the massive Windy Hill mast **15** (a television reflector station), and down along the stone-slabbed path to the M62.

The trans-Pennine motorway was opened after the Pennine Way, and an elegant footbridge **16**, built especially for the purpose, carries walkers over the obstacle.

Just after the bridge, take a path to bear left (west) along a wide track which soon veers north-west. Continue along this track for around 300 metres before descending slightly to the left. Now follow the stone-slabbed path to gain the heights of Blackstone Edge. This is a better route than the original Way over Slippery Moss.

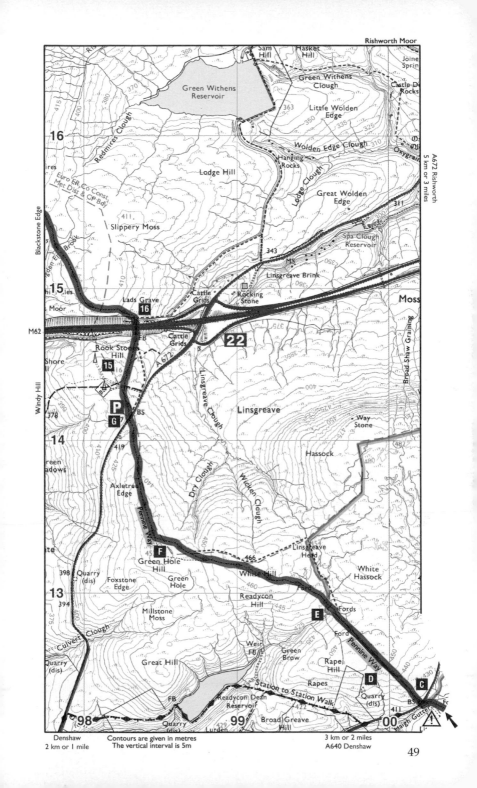

Rishworth Moor

A672 Rishworth
5 km or 3 miles

Sam Hill
Hasket Hill
Joine Sprin
Castle D
Rocks

Green Withens Reservoir

Green Withens Clough

Little Wolden Edge

Wolden Edge Clough

16

Redmires Clough

Lodge Hill

Hanging Rocks

Lodge Clough

Great Wolden Edge

Oxgrain

Blackstone Edge

Eden Brook

Euro GR Co Const Met Dist & CP Bdy

Slippery Moss

Spa Clough Reservoir

Linsgreave Brink

MS

15

Lads Grave

Cattle Grids

Rocking Stone

16

Moor

Moss

M62

Rook Stones Hill

Cattle Grids

22

Broad Shaw Graining

Windy Hill

15

A672

Shore

P

G 7

BS

Linsgreave

Way Stone

14

Axletree Edge

Pennine Way

Dry Clough

Wicken Clough

Hassock

13

Green Hole Hill

Green Hole

F

White Hill

466

Linsgreave Head

White Hassock

Quarry (dis)

Foxstone Edge

Readycon Hill

445

Fords

E

Culvert Clough

Millstone Moss

Ford

Pennine Way

Quarry (dis)

Great Hill

Weir FB

Green Brow

Rape Hill

D

Quarry (dis)

C

BS

FB

Station to Station Walk

Readycon Dean Reservoir

Rapes

98

Quarry (dis)

Lurden

99

Broad Greave Hill

00

Naigh Gutte

Denshaw
2 km or 1 mile

Contours are given in metres
The vertical interval is 5m

3 km or 2 miles
A640 Denshaw

49

Off Blackstone Edge and the Pennines towards Littleborough and Rochdale: a busy

landscape best viewed from afar.

Blackstone Edge **17** is comparable with Standedge, but the black stones are generally bigger and strewn over a larger area. Celia Fiennes, who toured the country on horseback at the end of the 17th century and kept a diary of her adventures, describes this as a 'dismal high precipice', and so it sometimes appears, but it also marks the start of much easier terrain for the walker. The triangulation pillar **18** stands on a broad whaleback of rock at an altitude of 1,549 feet (472 metres), the highest point on this section of the Way. There are good views east, over Green Withens Reservoir and West Yorkshire, and west, across Rochdale and Bolton. Ahead lies level, wide moorland, more reservoirs and a scatter of pylons. Soon after passing the triangulation pillar, leave the ridge crest and pick your way around great loaf-shaped blocks of gritstone, then follow the well-marked path on the Lancashire side of the moor. The path descends slightly, then undulates through a boulder field. Sections of the field have been surfaced with local gritstone to give an experimental 'causey' finish. Eventually you reach and go through a kissing gate on to a track.

This is an ancient cross-Pennine route and is marked on maps as a Roman road. Daniel Defoe rode along it in the 1720s, and was suitably impressed. In places the broad, cobbled or flagged surface is remarkably preserved, but whether it is of Roman or medieval origin is obscure, and open to debate. This part of the Pennines is a maze of trackways, often packhorse trails created in the early 18th century. Since landowners were responsible for the maintenance of any routes across their land, they were not enthusiastic about this increase and began, by the middle of the century, to build turnpike roads instead. Directly across the track, on the brow of the moor, is a small standing stone **19** marked with a cross and the initials I.T. This is the Aiggin Stone, probably a landmark for the crossing of Blackstone Edge on the ancient road, but its origins are equally obscure. The Pennine Way follows the 'Roman road' down the hill to the west. Its rough stone surface soon changes to the well-engineered stone paving for which it is famous. This was once known as the 'Dhoul's Pavement' – the Devil's pavement. After a few hundred yards, cross the small footbridge over Broad Head Drain. Then turn right (north) **H** along a 2-metre-wide track and follow this until you reach a gate. Turn downhill to the left (west): this leads to the A58 (Sowerby Bridge–Littleborough) road. Cross with care.

After turning right on the road, past the White House Inn **20**, the Way soon turns left along a track beside Blackstone Edge

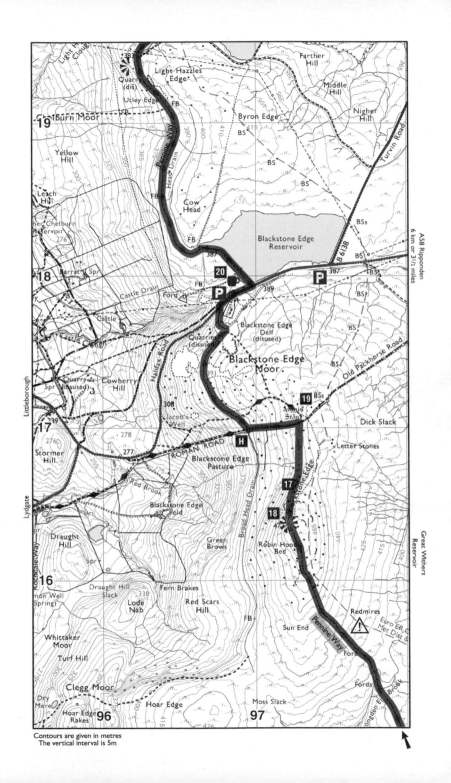

Contours are given in metres
The vertical interval is 5m

Reservoir. The grassy bank below the dam wall, dotted with eyebright and clover, contrasts with the natural vegetation of the uplands. After the end of the reservoir keep with the wide sandy track and follow a spillway called the Head Drain. The verges here are dominated by purple moor grass (*Molinia*), whose oily dark seedheads give the plant a mauve or purple colour when seen from a distance in summer. During the winter the stems and leaves turn brittle, and in strong winds the litter is blown across the moors – hence the local name 'flying bent'. The going is level. Beyond Utley Edge there is a view down Light Hazzles Clough and the headwaters of the River Roch, over the valley of the Rochdale Canal and Calderbrook, with hay meadows and moorland beyond.

The Way continues along the trackway (not right along the waymarked circuit of reservoirs) under electricity pylons, and beside Light Hazzles Reservoir. Like its neighbours at Blackstone Edge, White Holme and Warland this was built to provide the water for the Rochdale Canal, which opened in 1804.

You now follow the Warland Drain, with the Holder Stones on the skyline to the south-east, but where the Drain flows sharp right **I** (south-east), you turn northwards and head along the stone-slabbed path over Lang Field Common (an old urban common), taking a line slightly to the right of the rock-strewn dome of Coldwell Hill. From the cairn there are good views all around, but attention now is focused on Stoodley Pike, the broad, needle-shaped monument on the hilltop to the north-east.

The descent northwards from Coldwell Hill is straightforward; the path is clear and not very boggy, and there are excellent views of the tree-lined Calder valley. At the bottom of the hill the Pennine Way crosses the Calderdale Way at Withens Gate **J**; a very obvious causey of sandstone flags leads downhill to the west, to Mankinholes and Todmorden. Mankinholes Youth Hostel provides a possible overnight stop, an alternative to Hebden Bridge. To the east, the Calderdale Way follows the old packhorse route to Cragg Vale. In the 18th century this area was the refuge of the Yorkshire Coiners, who made a living from clipping the edges of foreign coins and counterfeiting sovereigns with the pieces.

About 250 yards from the crossroad of the Ways stands the 'Te Deum Stone', marked with a cross and probably denoting the highest point of a 'corpse road', where coffin-bearers could rest on their way to the burial ground.

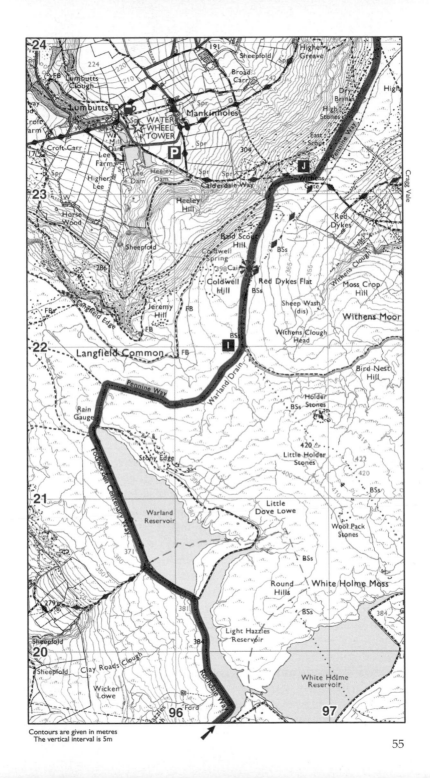

Contours are given in metres
The vertical interval is 5m

55

Beech trees on the slopes of Calderdale.

From Withens Gate **J**, you follow the hill crest of Higher Moor up to Stoodley Pike **21**. There was a tower or pike on the hill top in the early 18th century, but it was the defeat of Napoleon in 1814 that prompted the erection of a 115-foot (35-metre) monument to peace. Unfortunately, Napoleon escaped from Elba in 1815 and work was postponed. It was completed shortly after the Battle of Waterloo. In 1854 the whole thing collapsed; the present very solid tower was built two years later and stands about 125 feet (38 metres) tall.

From Stoodley Pike and its nearby viewpoint cairn, you head down a clear, wide path in the direction of a plantation, through a squeeze-stile in a wall, then turn left over a ladder-stile **K** and make your way steeply downhill. After open moorland the countryside now seems much softer, composed of pastures and meadows grouped around cottages. Most of the enclosures date back to the early 19th century, but corrugations in the pasture above denote much older field systems.

If you are intending to stop at Hebden Bridge there is a walled lane (Kilnshaw Lane) that heads to the town from the Swillington turn. To follow the Pennine Way, turn left at a wall, right beside a field, then out to a walled track beside Lower Rough Head Farm **22**. Further down, follow the track through a beautiful little wood, very wet and therefore very green, with alder, birch, willow and a few oaks and wych-elms. Marsh thistle, celery-leaved buttercup, rosebay, meadowsweet and hemlock water-dropwort are a few of the early summer flowers. By the roadside, on the drier banks, there are foxgloves and bluebells.

Past Edge End Farm most of Callis Wood is oak and birch, the summer home of redstarts and wood warblers. Nearby is a medieval deer park and the unusual 17th-century model farm of Errington Grange. Ahead, through the trees and on a hill on the far side of the Calder valley, is Heptonstall Church. Soon you bear left (west) along the track and then turn right **L** to cross the Rochdale Canal and the River Calder. Hebden Bridge and the cradle-land of British industry is suddenly close at hand. You can walk into the town along the towpath for an overnight stay.

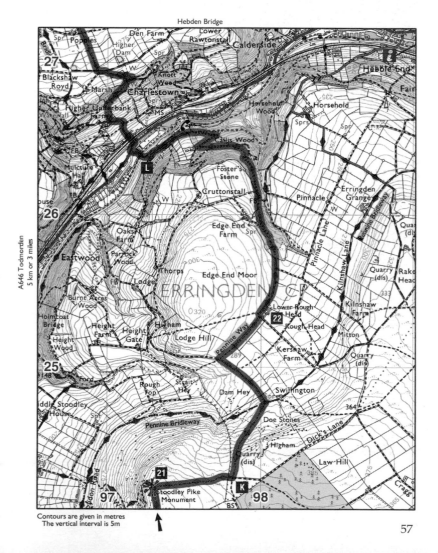

Hebden Bridge

Contours are given in metres
The vertical interval is 5m

CIRCULAR WALK: MANKINHOLES AND CALDERDALE

13¹/₂ miles (21.7 km)

The excellent stretch of the Pennine Way approaching Calderdale links with the more recently established Calderdale Way to make an impressive circular walk, with some *steep climbs* up the valley stages rewarded by outstanding views.

From Mankinholes, where it is possible to park near Lumbutts Chapel, the route heads south to pick up the Calderdale Way above Lee and Heeley Dams. From here there is a *sharp climb* eastwards on a packhorse trail to meet the Pennine Way on the shoulder of the hill at Withens Gate. The route then follows the Pennine Way northwards, past Stoodley Pike **21** and through Callis Wood into Calderdale. Pass under the railway bridge, turn left and walk alongside the embankment. At the stream turn right and follow it for about 500 yards. Cross the

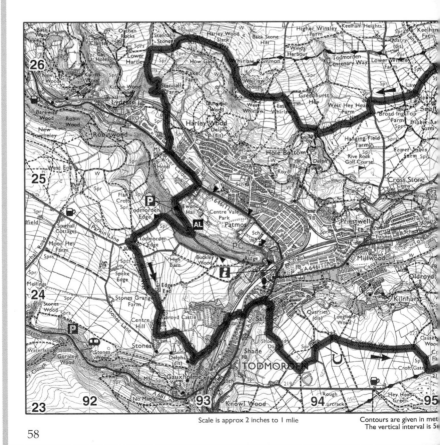

Scale is approx 2 inches to 1 mlie

Contours are given in met
The vertical interval is 5i

footbridge and continue up Jumble Hole Clough with the stream on your right. Cross again near Hippins and rejoin the Calderdale Way, which passes Staups Dam and Whirlaw Common to drop down into the Calder valley above Todmorden. After following the A646(T) for a short distance along the Calderdale Way turn south-west along a side road, then strike up the *steep* wooded slope of Todmorden Edge. Head south before bearing east, dropping down into another valley to cross the Rochdale Canal. A short walk along the A6033 and a last *climb* out of the valley then leads over fields to Lumbutts and back to Mankinholes.

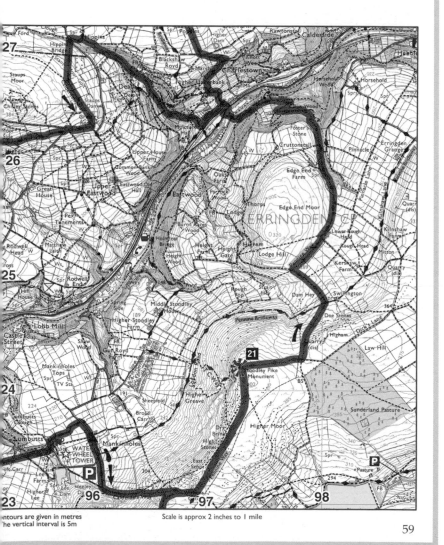

ntours are given in metres
he vertical interval is 5m

Scale is approx 2 inches to 1 mile

Hebden Bridge, a town of terraces following one of the most important cross- Penni

Hebden Bridge

Overnighting in Hebden Bridge may not be a joyous prospect for long-distance walkers, but any prejudice against mill-towns should be dispelled by its warm welcome. Hebden is full of shops, cafés, restaurants, pubs and accommodation.

Until the beginning of the 19th century it had little more than its packhorse bridge and a nearby inn called the Hole in the Wall. In those days Heptonstall was the main community, a hilltop village inhabited by farm-workers and handloom weavers. The Industrial Revolution changed things dramatically. Water-power and communications concentrated development in the Calder valley and its tributaries, a string of cotton mills sprang up, serviced by a turnpike road, a canal, then a railway; Hebden grew steadily and became an interna-

routes.

tional centre for the fustian trade (fustian is a thick-twilled, short-napped, cotton cloth such as a corduroy). The town reached its prosperous, confident, and very dirty heyday in the early years of the 20th century; the sooty walls remain to tell the tale. Foreign competition killed off the town's industrial base, the Hole in the Wall was demolished following a protracted campaign by temperance groups, but there are still 'double-decked' houses stacked up the steep hill terraces and a host of bridges and mill buildings along the river and the Rochdale Canal. The view of the town from the Pennine Way is fleeting and incomplete. The route crosses the valley to the west of the main settlement and a detour is necessary if anything more is to be seen of the place, but it is a natural starting and finishing point and is well served by buses and trains.

4 Hebden Bridge to Ponden

past Heptonstall Moor and Walshaw Dean Reservoirs
10³/₄ miles (17.3 km)

After miles on the rooftop of England you now find yourself down in the boiler-room, crossing a ribbon of road, rail, canal, river, and industrial terraces.

From the main road **A**, 1¹/₂ miles (2.5 km) west of Hebden Bridge, this section of the Pennine Way climbs quickly and quite steeply through pastures and meadows, descends to cross the pretty Colden Water, then climbs to open heather moorland and, via the Walshaw Dean Reservoirs, reaches its highest point at Withins ('Wuthering Heights'), and goes down through pastures to Ponden Reservoir near Haworth. It is straightforward and attractive – there are few bogs, and the walls and sheep are no longer covered in soot.

The route is signed from the A646(T), along a track called Underbank Avenue, starting in the shade of tall sycamores and heading north, under the railway bridge. The line was originally built for the Lancashire and Yorkshire Railway. Further up, as the walled and cobbled track bears left, look back over the valley and gain a good impression of how industry made a heavy mark on what was, until the early 19th cen-

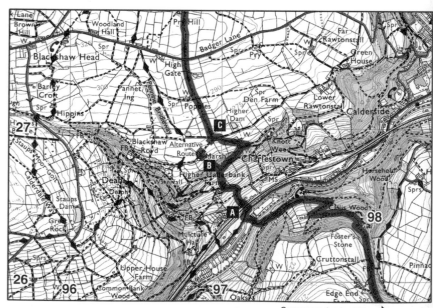

Contours are given in metres
The vertical interval is 5m

tury, a farming community. There are blackened terraces of workers' houses with (now) brightly coloured paintwork, but also barns and byres. Across the valley you can see Stoodley Pike and the Pennine Way descent through Callis Wood – and the sewage works at the foot of the slope.

Soon, pasture and woodland appear to the right of the track. Past a derelict building, and just before a curious little abutment with railings and a small square tower (actually a ruined chapel with a little graveyard), you turn sharp right **B**. There are two alternatives signposted; left on a Wainwright route, or keep on the official route. The latter contours along the hillside, keeping on level ground for some way beside an old pasture full of thistles and ragwort (both plants thrive on neglect). You begin to rise and the vegetation turns heathy, with patches of heather, until you reach some steps next to a little waterfall in a square stone column (actually a long-drop loo). From here the Way continues along a track around farm buildings (partly derelict), and on a walled track to an oblique junction at more buildings, at which the route bears left. After about 100 yards there is a gap in a wall on the right, and you at last head north on a grassy path **C**. Most of the enclosures in this area are square or oblong, a geometric grid imposed on the commons towards the end of the 18th century.

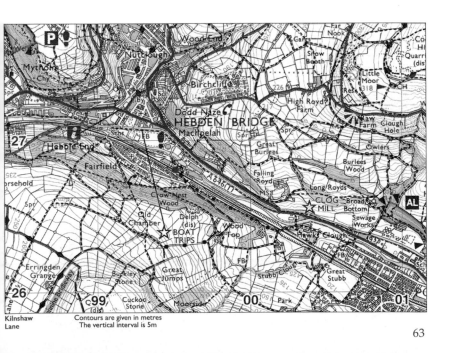

Kilnshaw
Lane

Contours are given in metres
The vertical interval is 5m

63

After heading north over more fields, across a road and over Pry Hill, you descend into the Colden Valley on a narrow path, crossing a beautiful heather-lined track, with views to the right of the widening Colden Clough and Heptonstall Church (where the poet Sylvia Plath is buried). You go down a steep bank of heather and bilberry, and make for an old pack-horse bridge at Hebble Hole **23**, which takes both the Pennine Way and the Calderdale Way over Colden Water.

Dippers and grey wagtails find the stream to their liking; they both feed their young on insects, but the dipper, despite its unlikely shape, dives for larvae, while the wagtail picks them from among the shoreline pebbles. Wagtails are among the most beautiful and elegant of waterside birds; both the pied and grey wagtails are resident but move down to the lowlands only to avoid severe weather.

The slabbed Calderdale Way now heads east, leaving the Pennine Way to climb steeply uphill, bearing left around Goose Hey Farm and north again to meet the Burnley–Hebden Bridge road **D**. A little further on, you cross a smaller side road. High Gate Farm shop lies 250 yards (230 metres) to the left.

The track is firm and clear as you cross a brow before descending obliquely to a walled field corner, on the shoulder of Hot Stones Hill, with a ruined farm building across the field to the right. The path ahead veers gradually left, north-east, up Clough Head Hill. There is a fine, featureless view all around, without pylons or poles and with few houses or trees. The going is mainly over tussocky grass rather than heather and the path is cairned every now and then, but not very clearly. Generally the terrain is easy and there are stone clapper-bridges over the worst of the marshy hollows. The path loses height gradually. Standing Stone Hill rises to the left (south-west) and to the right the ground falls away to Hebden Dale and Hardcastle Crags. To the north, in a cleft in the open hills, lie Walshaw Dean Reservoirs.

You follow a wall-fence down towards Gorple Lower Reservoir, then turn right down a track and through a gate to the reservoir houses. Cross straight over the reservoir access road and head downhill on a slabbed causey path into a rocky hollow **E** where the Reaps Water meets Graining Water. After crossing two footbridges, continue left above Graining Water, up a wide-slabbed track and alongside a wall, until a narrow walled track leads right to the road. Ignoring the step-stile to the right, turn left and past Well Hole Cottage and the entrance

Contours are given in metres
The vertical interval is 5m

to the Gorple reservoirs. Further on lies another of Yorkshire Water's reservoirs above Calderdale, called Widdop (the word is derived from 'wide valley'), but you turn sharp right **F** off the road just after the entrance drive to the Gorple reservoirs.

The route is signed, uphill and along a grassy path, then a concrete road. Turn right, down to the dam wall of Walshaw Dean Lower Reservoir **24**. Cross the dam wall and turn left, following a path above the reservoir shore. Although the reservoir is stone-sided and lacks any vegetation (other than rhododendrons), Walshaw Dean attracts some bird life including pied wagtail, mallard and Canada goose. Seeing a skein of geese flighting across the moors is an impressive sight, even if the Canada is not a native species.

Pass the dam wall of the middle reservoir **G**, along a path between the reservoir and a concrete spillway. The path leads to a walled bridge, where it turns left **H** over the bridge and through a gate (or over the adjacent stile), then right uphill through good heather along a causey or stone-slabbed path that was put in by the Calderdale Countryside Service in 1989.

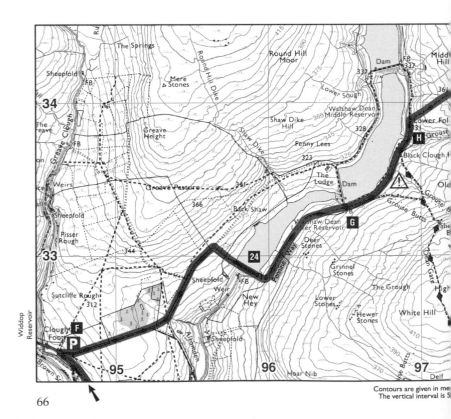

Contours are given in me
The vertical interval is 5

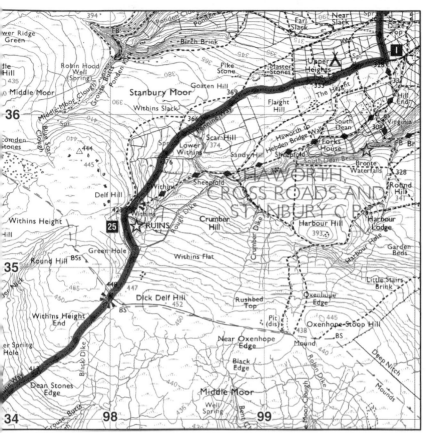

ontours are given in metres
The vertical interval is 5m

Continue uphill along a stone-slabbed path to a hill brow, from where all three of the Walshaw Dean Reservoirs are visible to the south-west, and due south is distant Stoodley Pike. Ahead and to the left is a broken spine of a wall leading to the ruins of Top Withins **25** (marked on OS maps as Withins). Readers of *Wuthering Heights* may be disappointed by the first sight of this famous ruin, which has been 'conserved', but the view from the lonely steading is still wonderful.

After passing Top Withins the Way drops downhill along a well-worn literary trail, passing levelled ruins (more Withins). Following the track, you eventually bear east-north-east and pass Upper Heights farm. Look for its date-mark (1761) and a mysterious face above the door. Below this the track forks. Bear left along the main track and past Lower Heights farm, then turn left off the track **I** to join the Brontë Way on a wide-walled grassy track, heading down from the moor and veering right **J** to Buckley Green (with another date-mark). Most Pennine Way walkers take a short cut straight downhill here, along a steep grassy path, then left on the track at the bottom towards Buckley House. Just before the house you bear right over a stile, down a sunken path, then continue through old pastures past a derelict barn and a farm to the right to the dam wall of Ponden Reservoir. Now you have a choice: either go straight on to the road and right, to Haworth 2 miles (3.5 km) away, or left to keep to the Pennine Way. If you choose the latter, the route follows a private road beside the reservoir then up to Ponden Hall **26**. It was built in 1680, extensively restored in 1801, and reputedly was the inspiration for Emily Brontë's Thrushcross Grange. Nearby Ponden House offers bed and breakfast accommodation and camping facilities. Follow the track past the outbuildings then contour north high above the reservoir until a turn to the right leads sharply downhill, over a bridge **K** at the head of the reservoir and so to the Colne–Haworth Road.

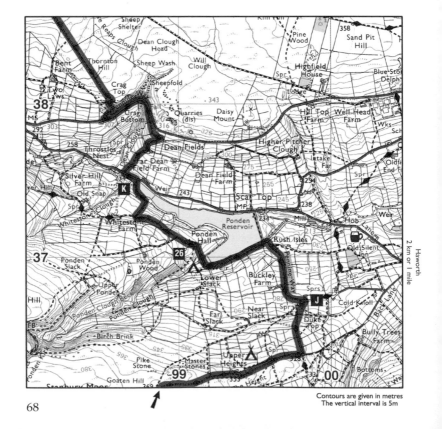

Contours are given in metres
The vertical interval is 5m

The Brontës of Haworth

Haworth will always be remembered as the home of the Brontës, a sensitive and gifted family growing up in the repressed and stifling setting of an early-19th-century parsonage. Their mother died when they were still young and their father, originally from Ireland, was poor and aloof. The family was raised by an austere aunt; their only escape was to imagine fantasy worlds and explore the local countryside.

Of the six Brontë children, the elder two sisters died of tuberculosis, contracted at a draconian girls' school at Cowan Bridge. Charlotte and Emily, who had been sent to the same school, returned home to Haworth to while away their youth in the company of brother Branwell and younger sister Anne. Although Charlotte tried to make her way as a governess or teacher, the family was firmly tied to Haworth. The girls escaped into writing; they had a book of poems published, at their own expense, which sold two copies. Their romantic novels fared much better. Emily's *Wuthering Heights*, Anne's *Agnes Grey* and Charlotte's *Jane Eyre* were all published in 1847. For Charlotte it brought instant recognition, but only fleeting happiness. In less than two years Branwell, Anne and Emily died of tuberculosis. Six years of literary success, coupled with personal loneliness and frustration, followed for Charlotte. She married her father's curate in 1854 but died in pregnancy a few months later.

The parsonage at Haworth is often described as a cold, grey house in a dour Pennine village. Neither is really true, and today Haworth is alive with shops and cafés. Top Withins, the inspiration for *Wuthering Heights*, beckons the more committed. Its setting is splendid and it should stir the imagination, but one of the most attractive things about a ruin is that it is insubstantial. It is a pity to see the once-crumbling remains of Top Withins enshrined as a blockhouse.

The descent into the Worth valley, with Ponden Reservoir in the distance.

71

5 Ponden to Thornton-in-Craven

through Cowling and Lothersdale
11¹/₂ miles (18.5 km)

Most walkers will begin this section from Haworth, in which case it is a good idea to start early to make up the 2¹/₂ miles (4 km) back to Ponden Reservoir. A grey day may lie ahead, over moors and mires and through the gritstone villages of Ickornshaw and Lothersdale, but by evening there will be green fields and firm footing to guide you into Thornton. The best of the Pennine Way will then brighten any gloom.

From the head of Ponden Reservoir, where the Pennine Way meets the Colne road **A**, the route heads west along the road, then across a stone step-stile right; you head uphill along a grassy path with Dean Clough to the left. The house in the sheltered cleft is called Throstles Nest, the name being derived from the Old English for song thrush. Place names often reflect the character of the countryside and its inhabitants, and in the uplands the song thrush is a bird of leafy bowers, implying a happy home. (The old name for the missel thrush is 'stormcock', implying something rather more appropriate to the high Pennines.)

Follow the path through a gap in the wall, then over the pastureland of Dean Fields. The exact route is waymarked. After passing to the right of a ruined barn, bear left along a track and over a stile, then on past a house to the right and along a walled track. Once past another set of old gateposts you turn sharp left, off the farm track, and walk beside an old wall-line to a step-stile. Then walk alongside a wall with a wood to the left until you reach a road. Turn left here to go over Crag Bottom at the head of Dean Clough. The road is shaded by sycamores, beeches and some wych-elms, and between the wall and the bridge face on the left-hand side of the road is a shady, damp spot where buckler ferns flourish. Among the normal woodland flowers are patches of American willowherb, a pretty little alien with pink flowers and broad short-stalked leaves.

After the bridge continue along the road until you reach Old Crag Bottom farm **27** (most notable for its fine mullioned windows). Turn right off the road and climb to Crag Top, from where there is a good view back to the farm, and beyond to the reservoir and the far slopes of the Worth Valley.

The route is signed over a fence-stile and north, with a wall to the left, to Thornton Hill. The vegetation quickly takes on a familiar Pennine look, dominated by bilberry and with sinister

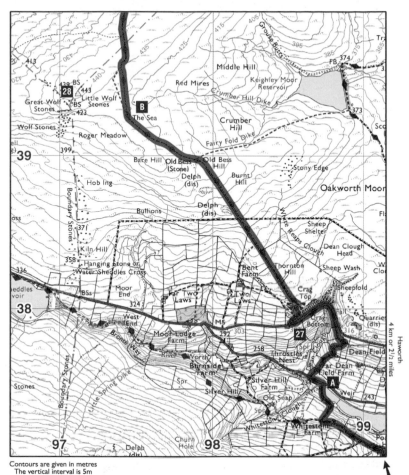

Contours are given in metres
The vertical interval is 5m

patches of rushes, which hint at the increasingly marshy nature
of the ground. Follow the wall, or fence and wall, until it ends
on Old Bess Hill. The path then becomes wide and clear and
you bear slightly left, uphill over open heather moorland. As it
levels off on to a wide hill crest, appropriately called The Sea,
you can see the triangulation pillar **28** at the Wolf Stones
directly ahead. There are many legends, and although it is
quite possible that wolves inhabited these hills in the 16th century, it is also possible that stories were invented simply to
keep children away from the moors.

Bear right **B** before you reach the pillar and pass to the left of
a shallow peaty pond, then follow the stone-flagged path, heading into the Craven District of North Yorkshire. The ground is
very boggy on either side, but underfoot the going is easy. This

is Ickornshaw Moor, inhabited by grouse and a few curlew and golden plover, but not a place to stop for a closer look as care is needed with route-finding. At a cairn bear left **C**, north-west, parallel to a deep channel, then turn north across an expanse of blanket bog full of runnels and wet flushes. The surface water drains down Cat Stone Hill.

The 'Cat' refers to wildcats which, like wolves, may have taken refuge here in the 16th and 17th centuries. In those days any wild animal was assumed to be hostile to farmers and their flocks, and most of the larger predators had a price on their heads. As their numbers diminished, it became easier to track the remaining outlaws to their final refuges on the wild moors; hence there are many stories of the elimination of martens, pole-cats, wildcats and wolves. The fox, of course, survived, perhaps because of its adaptability and cunning, perhaps because it became an object of sport and therefore received some measure of protection. In recent years the polecat has made a comeback in northern England. Not so the wildcat or wolf!

Eventually the path becomes more sandy and leads past a stone wind-shelter. The close-cropped grass around the hut **D** offers a comfortable seat and an excellent view. Peat has been dug here for centuries to provide fuel for cottages and farms in the valley to the north. Old pits scar the basin of the moor and there are some recent diggings close to the hut. Piles of drying peat bear witness to the timeless drudgery of the place.

Pen-y-ghent is now in sight far to the north, and to the east, on the top of the gritstone edge above Cowling, stand two monu-ments, Wainman's Pinnacle and Lund's Tower. From the hut **D** the route continues north over a low hill brow and down a clear path beside a wall, past several small wooden huts or chalets. Follow the path, bearing sharp left after a wall-stile and downhill again, still beside a dry stone wall and on an easy, grassy path.

At the end of the wall continue downhill following marked posts leading to a ladder-stile over a wall. The view now is of an enclosed landscape of green meadows and pastures, with Cowling Parish Church framed by trees in a cleft in the hills ahead. After the stile the path bears sharp left beside a wall, down past a ruined farm to cross a stream (Andrew Gutter) at a footbridge **E**. This is a world of derelict farmhouses, and it is easy to understand why the tenants decided to opt for life in the mill towns.

After a footbridge, skirt Eller Hill to the waterfall at Lumb Head. Circle above the waterfall. Lumb is the name of the farmhouse over the wall to the left. Continue along a walled track, straight on rather than left, along the more gravelled track of Lumb Lane, and drop down a 'green road', past Lower Summer House, a little farm stocked with a chaotic mixture of chickens, cats and sheep.

Over a stile in a wall head north down a track, then over a wall again and down through a pasture. In the damper places, and at the right time of year, there are violets and bluebells, lady-smock and stitchwort, and skylarks sing overhead. By keeping to single file it is possible to avoid trampling any potential hay crop while seeing the best of the flowers.

When you reach the A6068, turn left and then right, just before the Black Bull **29**. Take care when crossing the road;

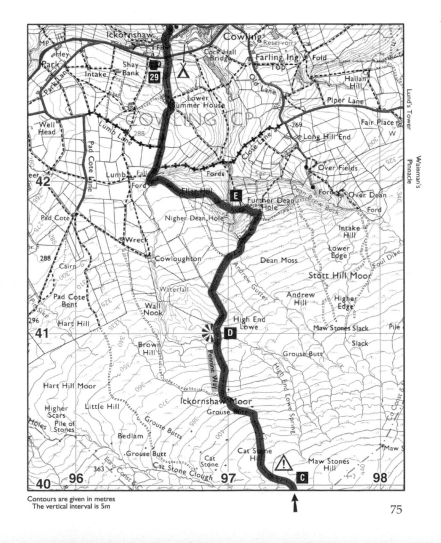

Contours are given in metres
The vertical interval is 5m

there is usually fast-moving traffic. Head downhill on a causey path to another road. Ickornshaw is an interesting little village but the Way does not linger and there are many miles to go. To continue turn right along the road, then bear left up a metalled track, past houses and along the edge of a field. Pass the edge of a singular terrace of houses, following a wall beside a meadow, then turn right, through the wall to a road. Go left along the road, and bear right where the road forks, and descend to Gill Bridge.

After the bridge the Way turns left and then, before a house, right along a track, through a stile by a gate, then sharp right and uphill through meadowland. Initially follow the grassy path beside a little stream with watercress, lady-smock and brooklime clothing its flanks. Away from the wettest ground there are banks of bluebells and primroses which, in the cool shade of the Pennine valleys, often last well into the summer. They are woodland plants and their presence on open grassland shows a surprising resilience; they have survived in precisely the same place for several thousand years despite the removal of the original tree cover. A continued absence of herbicides will probably be the key to their fortunes.

For the next $1^1/_4$ miles (2 km) the route passes through enclosed farmland along easy paths linking Low Stubbing and the derelict High Stubbing (the route is to the left of the buildings). Where the path meets a road F, turn right and then left (north-east) towards Over House. Continue until the road turns sharp right, where you go over a stile G and into fields to pass Woodhead Farm. Shortly after this the path forks and the right-hand route leads steeply downhill, beside a wall, to Lothersdale where there is a post office-shop 30.

Turn right along the road over a bridge and into the village of Lothersdale. After the Hare and Hounds Inn turn left through a farmyard and up a track, keeping to the left beside the remains of a hedge. The route now heads through more enclosed pastureland along clear paths. After crossing a road, head north-west along a concrete track and, when this turns left to Hewitts Farm, cross the wall and head uphill, first along a walled track, then over a field. Across a stile H the route heads west (left).

Moorland lies ahead, this time not the ooze of Ickornshaw but the sandy paths and heather of Elslack Moor leading to Pinhaw Beacon, on easy ground and with views opening out all around as you gain height to the summit at 1,273 feet (388

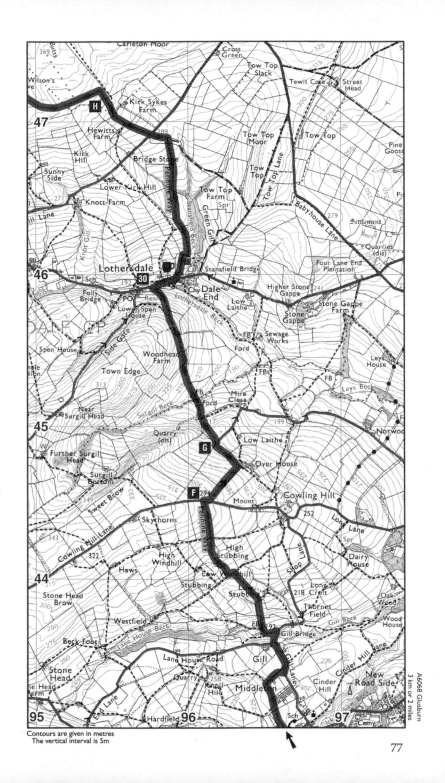

Contours are given in metres
The vertical interval is 5m

metres), marked by a triangulation pillar **31**. Here the Pennine Chain enters its middle third. Descend on a clear path to the humps and hollows of an old quarry, then down a track in the direction of the mast. When you reach a road (Colne to the south-west, Carleton to the north-east) cross directly and follow a smaller road north-west with moorland on either side.

The road that you are on (Clogger Lane) descends towards Elslack, but where a wall on the left bears away from the road **I**, the Way passes through a gate and stile and heads downhill, keeping the wall to the right, through a wonderfully remote place. After a wall-stile descend, through enclosures and over marshy ground (marsh rather than bog – there is a difference), until you bear right over a footbridge. Parts of the path are now

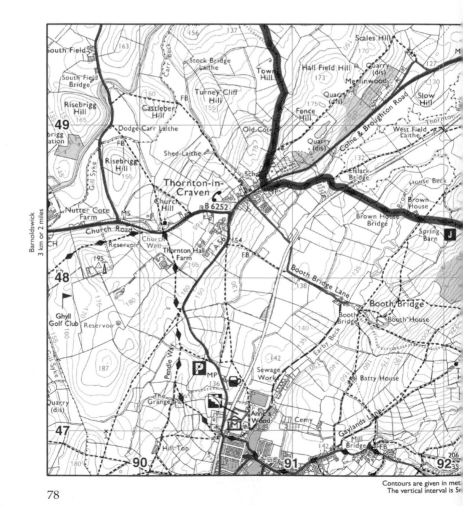

Contours are given in met
The vertical interval is 5t

stone-slabbed. For a while route-finding is straightforward. Head downhill with a farm away to your right, and on towards Thornton and its verdant valley. Cross a stile beside a gate, and continue on a broad grassy path past oak trees, then turn obliquely away from the wall on the brow of the bank above the stream, over a stile and down through pastureland. After a stile in a field corner **J** the route leads down to Brown House Farm (take care not to mistake this for the nearby barn conversion – Spring Barn). A stile leads the Pennine Way through the farmyard, past the farmhouse and to a metalled track.

The rest of the route is easy along the track into the valley, under a bridge beneath the old railway, and uphill into Thornton-in-Craven.

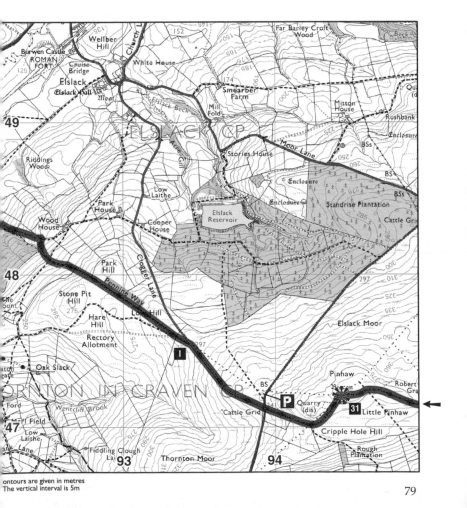

ontours are given in metres
The vertical interval is 5m

The heather that was once abundant on the moorlands is now being actively encouraged again, as a habitat for the red grouse.

Heather and the red grouse

Over most of Britain the common heather *Calluna vulgaris* takes the dominant role in plant communities of acidic moorland. Purple hillsides have become a cliché for the beauty of the uplands, but in most places there has been a widespread loss of heather caused by the overstocking of sheep and a decrease in grouse management.

Red grouse rely on heather, which protects them from severe weather and from predators, and forms more than three-quarters of their diet. When grouse shooting became the vogue in the 1850s, following the invention of the breech-loading shotgun, landowners invested a great deal of money in their moorland. They excluded sheep and over the following century a system of grouse husbandry was established. Patches of heather were burned on a rotational basis to create a mosaic of different-aged growth for feeding, roosting and nesting. Predators, such as foxes and hawks, were eliminated. The grouse found all this to their liking, and by the turn of the 20th century a stocking ratio of a bird per acre was the norm and bags of over 1,000 birds a day were common on all the best estates. Unfortunately overpopulation also brought a disease, *strongylosis*, and numbers eventually suffered a severe decline. Things never quite recovered. A precarious balance between heather, grouse, predators, keepers and landowners was maintained until the post-war decades, by which time the whole enterprise had become unfashionable and very costly. Gradually sheep were returned to the hills in much bigger numbers.

Recently there has been a revival of interest, and nature conservation groups have been trying to encourage the re-establishment of heather moorland as a wildlife habitat. Most Pennine Way walkers enjoy the company of grouse, particularly on dreary stretches of the route. The red grouse is a very British bird, solid, tetchy and conservative in habitats, but also restricted in distribution, a sub-species of the willow grouse found nowhere else in the world.

6 Thornton-in-Craven to Malham

through Gargrave and Airton
10¹/₂ miles (16.9 km)

An easy day rarely lives long in the memory, and the section of the Pennine Way from Thornton to Malham has neither high nor low points to exhilarate or depress the walker. It is a pleasant in-between part of the trail, beginning with rolling pastures and ending with a riverside walk.

Thornton-in-Craven is a pretty village with the busy A56 Colne–Skipton road running through it. The Pennine Way continues by heading north up Cam Lane **A**, past new or renovated cottages and some fine gardens. The route bears to the right of an attractive terrace of old cottages, then along what is now a track and to the left of Old Cote Farm. Green fields can be seen away to the left and ahead, in the hazy distance, stands Pen-y-ghent in the heart of the Yorkshire Dales National Park. After passing a barn to the left and going through a gate, you continue beside a hedge for about 45 yards (50 metres), then bear half-right **B** up a grassy path. This is a very pastoral landscape, the terrain is firm, and there is little trouble with route-finding. Once over the brow of Langber Hill you descend to a stile beside a group of ash trees, then climb again, through a gate, and right, along the towpath of the Leeds and Liverpool Canal **32**.

Like every canal built to serve industry by the quick and efficient movement of raw materials, the life of the Leeds and Liverpool Canal was busy but brief. During the 19th century it was a congested highway for shortboats, narrowboats and packetboats, all pulled by heavy horses, but the arrival of the railways made waterways less competitive, and by the 1920s there was obviously no future for canal transport. Recent developments in the leisure industry have given the Leeds and Liverpool Canal a new lease of life and it is neater now than it was in its heyday.

The route follows the towpath beneath a little bridge by a barn; the canal is wider here and provides an unofficial turning circle for 70-foot narrowboats. Swans nest each year in the reeds in front of East Marton Church. Around the next canal bend is another bridge (number 161) **33**, a curious double-arched affair supporting the A59 trunk road. The upper arch was built on top of the original bridge to raise its height and level the road for fast or heavy traffic. It is ironic that the canal itself became a nuisance to cross-Pennine commerce.

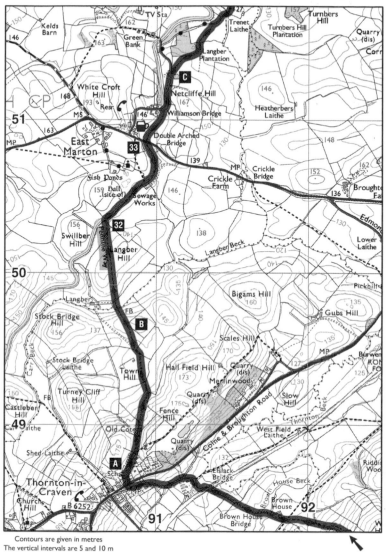

Contours are given in metres
The vertical intervals are 5 and 10 m

The deep cutting of the canal is shaded by beech and sycamore trees. North from the A59 the Way keeps to the towpath until it meets another bridge (Williamson Bridge) where it bears right, up the bank to meet a road. Keep to this little road past a pool to the right, then turn right **C** off the road through a squeeze-stile and over a pasture to another stile, then along a short path to skirt the edge of a beechwood. Beeches look magnificent but they have severe drawbacks for wildlife. The leaves form a dense canopy that blots out light, and in autumn when they fall they form a papery carpet that is slow to decay. Consequently the ground beneath beech trees is usually bare and lifeless, and even on the wood edge the only plants to thrive are species such as dog's mercury, which are tolerant of heavy shade. Every few years the trees produce a crop of seed (mast), and for a while the beechwoods become noisily alive with grey squirrels, wood-pigeons and jays enjoying the surfeit of food.

The Way heads north from the beechwood across a field to pass close to a crab-apple tree – a Goliath compared with the usual hedgerow examples. At a narrow lane you turn right, with the canal still a stone's throw away but this time above a grassy embankment and therefore invisible. Further along the lane and over a bridge, turn right at a stile **D** and head half-left, uphill on pastureland, over the brow with Turnbers Hill to the right, then down to Crickle Beck. This drains the surrounding fields but follows an ancient course, edged by marsh flowers such as brooklime, catmint and marsh marigold. You meet the beck again close to Newton Grange Farm. The fields here probably contain Ayrshire cattle, brown and white and smaller than Friesians, and once popular because they could fit into a traditional byre and their milk was good.

Further along the path the beck is fenced to protect young trees from browsing by stock; another sign of the times as conservation gains currency. Follow the Way across the beck at a stile **E** and head uphill (not right, which is the tempting line), obliquely away from the fence, on an indistinct path, to make for a wooded stile in a fenced hedgerow. From here, make for a post on the brow of the pasture, with Scaleber Hill to the left. There are better views now to the north across Airedale and the little town of Gargrave, then into the Yorkshire Dales National Park and the beginning of real limestone country. You descend into the wide valley, joining a concrete track that follows an ancient hedgerow, to cross a railway bridge. About 45 yards (50 metres) past the bridge, turn right **F** over a step-stile and head across fields and through a squeeze-stile in a wall into the outskirts of Gargrave. Turn right through a gate, and left along a road into the middle of the town. St Andrew's Church **34** is the most dominant feature – reputedly spared by the Scots during the border troubles because it was named after their patron saint.

At the end of the road the Way crosses the River Aire **35**, shallow and stony, like a large mountain stream. The Aire Gap is an important cross-Pennine route and shows many scars, from Roman marching camps and Norse settlements to derelict railway and petrol stations. It also carries the A65(T) road and much of the tourist traffic into the southern dales.

Once over the bridge and across the main road, the route heads north along a side road (the corner house bears the name 'Grouse'). After passing the village hall and car park bear left and a smaller road continues northwards, over the Leeds and Liverpool Canal. When this road turns right you again follow a narrower road, which continues north-west around Gargrave House and beside a wood.

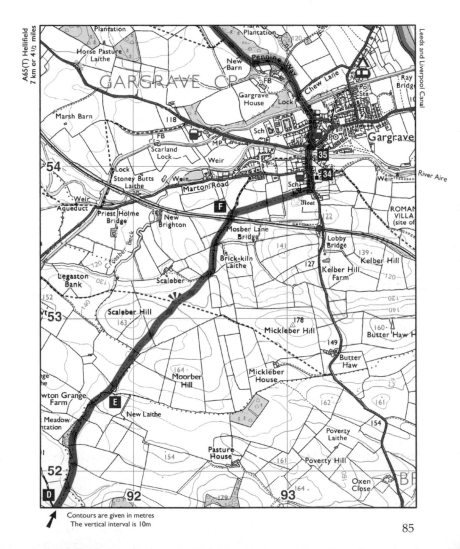

Contours are given in metres
The vertical interval is 10m

Just beyond this wood you bear right **G** up to a stile **H** through a wall, then take a path across a field. At first the path follows the track, leading to a stile in a field corner and then uphill to a post on the edge of an enclosure at Harrows Hill – still marked on the map as woodland but now felled. From here you continue north-west across rolling pastureland, down to a stile, then up a broad hill crest to meet a wall that marks the boundary of the Yorkshire Dales National Park. At the wall corner to the left **I** a gate and stile lead you right, north-west-wards again, and on a clear path downhill to cross several fields and stiles to a wall beside a road **J**. Now bear left at the wall, then go through a gate in another wall to the left, and walk over a footbridge across the River Aire, notably reduced in size because it now lies upstream of some of its feeder dykes and sikes. The character of the route changes completely as it follows the river northwards.

The Aire is delightful, providing the most attractive riverside sequence of the whole Pennine Way. In summer cattle wade in the shallows, beech and willow trees overhang the banks; there are carpets of cowslips and primroses. Grey wagtails, dippers and common sandpipers are always about, and the adjacent pastures attract redshank, curlews and lapwings. At Newfield Bridge **K** the Way crosses to the east bank, passing a weir and

The River Aire below Newfield Bridge, shaded by beech trees.

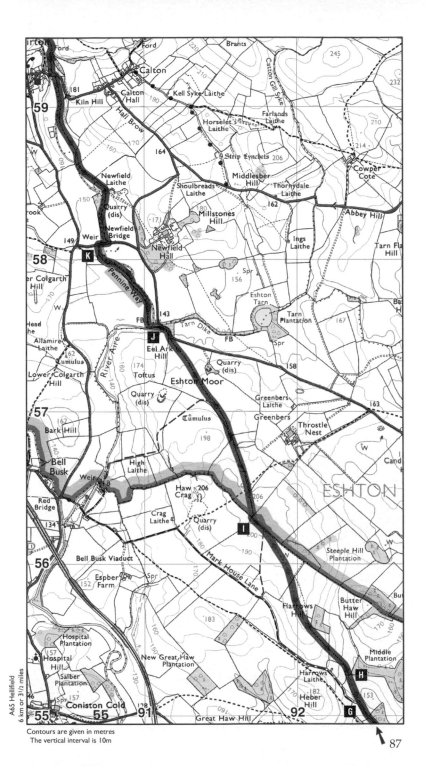

Contours are given in metres
The vertical interval is 10m

A65 Hellifield
6 km or 3½ miles

heading north to Airton **36**, a tiny village on the west side of the river clustered around a green on which stands a 'squatter's house' – a relic of the 17th century when a homeless person could apply to the Quarter Sessions for permission to build a house on common ground. Heading north again, still on the east bank, the old mill **37** once owned by the canons of Bolton Priory stands on the opposite bank, looking very smart and tidy, having been converted into residential accommodation.

Further north, the Way passes some good banks and crags covered with trees, with drifts of bluebells and other flowers. The river meanders and the path sometimes cuts off the curves, but the route is clear to the road at Hanlith. Leave the river bank at Hanlith Bridge **L** and turn right up the road past Badger House **38**, with its remarkable badger weather vane, and climb steeply uphill until the road turns left, then sharp right at a set of farm buildings (mostly converted into dwellings). Turn off the road here **M**, walk left through a small gate to the west side of the farm entrance. A series of low posts leads over the brow of a hill.

For the first time Malham Cove and Gordale Scar, which signal the dramatic exposure of the Great Scar Limestone at the Middle Craven Fault, seem very close and it is possible to appreciate both the limestone panorama and the fine detail that makes it such good walking country. Across the river valley to the left there are the marks of old terraces, or 'lynchets', a reminder that this has been farmland for thousands of years. Above, to the left and right, are moors and crags, less generous sweeps of country that have always been a challenge.

Soon you follow the Way as it descends to a wall-end, then bear right to a ladder-stile across a wall and angle north-east above a hanger of mixed deciduous trees. The view ahead now includes Malham village **39**, usually alive with tourists, and the route leads downhill to a stile **N** along a riverside path and into the village.

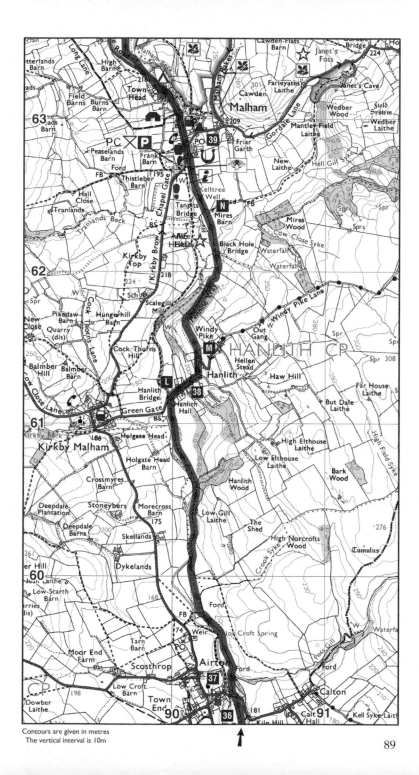

Contours are given in metres
The vertical interval is 10m

89

Limestone pavement

Garden walls around Dales cottages are often topped by a line of contorted limestone slabs, like pieces from a giant jigsaw. It is difficult to imagine where they come from, but above the hard-edged scars on the upper shoulder of the Dales valleys there are wide benches of this material, and between the cracks and crevices on its surface there are worlds within worlds where rare flowers thrive. Since Victorian times, when rock gardens became fashionable, hundreds of tons of limestone pavement have disappeared from the fells and found their way into village gardens, as have many of the flowers. Fortunately all limestone pavements in the National Park are now protected.

Rainwater, which contains some carbon dioxide from the atmosphere, dissolves limestone. Given time any exposed features will be melted away. When ice sheets retreated from the Dales they left flat shelves of white Great Scar Limestone. This started out as featureless surface rock, but after the ice came the rain. Water entered grooves, then channels, then clefts. Cavities were hollowed out and a mosaic of square-topped ridges and deep furrows was formed. There was no soil. As soon as rain fell it disappeared into the ground, feeding subterranean rivers, which created impressive cave systems. The surface remained as dry as bone.

The system of ridges and clefts is known locally as 'clints' and 'grikes', and the technical word for this sort of limestone country is 'karst' or glacial karst. The Yorkshire Dales show it at its very best: austere and inspiring. Sheep graze every hill, so most trees growing from the grikes are stunted and shorn. Those few ash, hazel and hawthorn bushes that escape their attention are beaten and gnarled by the wind. In a few places, such as Colt Park, enclosures keep out the sheep and a unique ash-dominated woodland has survived, showing what a natural landscape might look like. The ground flora on ungrazed clints includes globeflower, giant bellflower, bloody cranesbill and herb paris – a mix of mountain, grassland and woodland flowers. The grikes provide a safe, moist and sheltered enclave. Lily of the valley, angular Solomon's seal, dark-red helleborine, mountain avens, green spleenwort and holly fern are a few of the specialities.

It is easy to see why Victorians wanted to carry these enchanted rock gardens back home with them; it was a selfish age. Dull stones on garden walls are the legacy. So are the huge quarries that are eating into the Great Scar at Horton in Ribblesdale.

A pavement edge; the view south from the lip of the limestone pavement above Malham Cove.

91

7 Malham to Horton in Ribblesdale

around Malham Tarn and over Pen-y-ghent
14¹/₄ miles (22.9 km)

The village of Malham **39** has traded clogs and corduroy for rucksacks and brightly coloured Gore-tex. At the beginning of the 20th century it was a place of mines and mills, but it now caters almost exclusively for tourists and is one of the busiest villages in the Yorkshire Dales, two of the major attractions being the nearby cove and the tarn. This section of the Way includes both of these remarkable features, but you leave most of the daytrippers behind by heading north-west to the shoulder of dour Fountains Fell, then west across Silverdale and north up to the summit of Pen-y-ghent. From here there is a scenic descent into Horton in Ribblesdale. It is not strictly necessary to take in Pen-y-ghent, and in poor visibility it is probably a sensible idea to turn west to Brackenbottom before the steep pull to the summit. However, this is the most stunningly beautiful part of the whole walk.

Gordale Scar – off the Pennine Way route, but a popular detour for walkers.

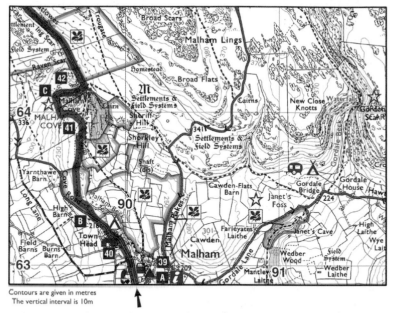

Contours are given in metres
The vertical interval is 10m

From Monk's Bridge **A**, close to the post office and the Buck Inn north of the main car park in Malham, the Way turns north along Cove Road (signposted 'Malham Tarn 3, Langcliffe 7, Settle 8'), which passes the village hall and some pretty cottages, then rises to a cluster of buildings at Town Head **40** which includes the old (17th-century) calamine store-house, used when this mineral was mined in the area. After Town Head you soon turn right **B**, off the road and along a gravel track. Your eyes will now be drawn to Malham Cove **41**, the arc of sheer 260-foot (80-metre) high limestone that lies ahead, but the green oasis before the famous cliff is worth a few minutes' contemplation. On the far side of Malham Beck a series of lynchets dates from the Dark Ages, and on the near side of the stream are the remains of an Iron Age settlement.

Follow the route along the ash-lined beck towards the rock face, then turn sharp left at a path junction to climb to the west shoulder of the cliff top. By continuing straight on from the junction it is possible to get to the very foot of the cliff. The steep, stepped path up the side of the cove leads to a kissing gate **C**, then you turn right to cross shelves of deeply eroded limestone pavement **42**. The route here crosses the top of the cliff and, without going too close to the edge, it is possible to take in a wonderful view of Malham Beck and village, and a distant panorama including Pendle Hill to the extreme right.

On the far side of the pavement follow the well-used path up the Watlowes Valley **43**. The landscape is arid and stony, the epitome of karst scenery. The route follows a dry stone wall, up the dry valley. At the top, cross a stile and go sharp right, then skirt Comb Hill **D**. Continue over the flat limestone grassland, by sink-holes and a stream which appears and disappears, depending on the time of year. Eventually you reach a road: cross this and skirt Tarn Foot along a clear path to a gate. This leads into the nature reserve of Malham Tarn **44**. The tarn, a respectable-sized lake, lies to the left, its beauty of the gentlest kind, resulting from the interplay between woodland and water. The natural tarn was extended in the late 18th century by Lord Ribblesdale, who also built the big house (as a shooting lodge) and planted the hill slopes with trees.

The Way follows the track around the tarn towards the wood above the north shore. Uphill to the right, across a saddle in the hills to the left of Great Close, lies the ancient Monk's Road **45**, a path used by the monks of Fountains Abbey when much of this area was grazed by their sheep. In the Middle Ages monks extended their sheep husbandry over much of upland Britain, and wool was a very valuable commodity. They were also adept at fish farming, and Malham Tarn became famous for its trout.

The Way follows the track through the wood. The big house **46** is now a Field Centre managed by the Field Studies Council. Once past the house the route continues along a broad track, with shady verge flora, including dog's mercury and enchanter's nightshade. The latter is not related to the true nightshades and is a delicate plant, often overlooked, with a sparse spike of tiny whitish flowers. By contrast dog's mercury is difficult to avoid; it forms dense carpets and is one of the first woodland plants to appear in spring, though the flowers themselves are small and green.

Just before a house on the right, turn right **E** through a gate off the track and on to a grassy path. You pass a line of sycamore and, uphill, a scatter of limestone boulders, then follow dry stone walls across several fields before veering left downhill across pastureland to a road. Directly across the road the route leads through a kissing gate **F** beside a cattle grid, then along a track to Tennant Gill Farm. Pass to the left of the farm and bear left before climbing to a ladder-stile.

Once over the stile you are on to the open fells, not 'sweet' limestone grasses but the 'sour' vegetation of sandstone moorland, and a hard climb lies ahead. Bear left then turn right to

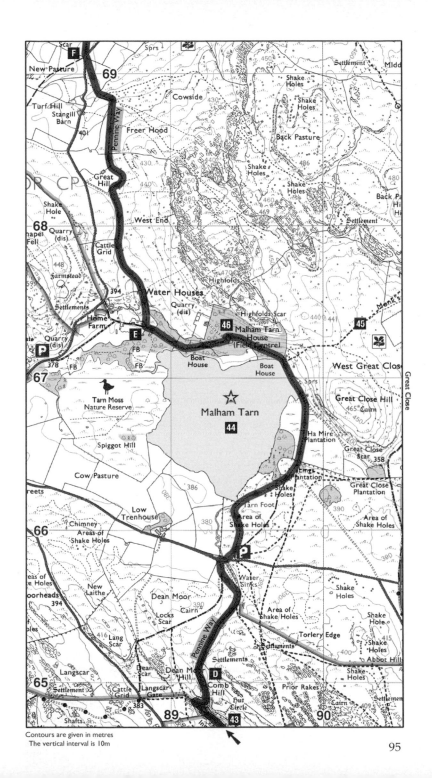

Contours are given in metres
The vertical interval is 10m

95

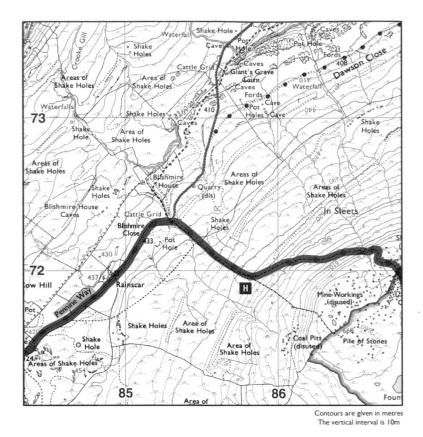

Contours are given in metres
The vertical interval is 10m

reach an old wall-line. After keeping straight for a while, angle
right and begin to climb, persistently, always keeping to the right
to avoid the steepest ground, following an old mine track and a
newly built path. The ground is sometimes boggy but there are
clapper-bridges over the worst parts around Tennant Gill **G**.

There are several false crests before the top of Fountains Fell is
reached. The actual summit **47** lies to the south-west, amid a
field of cairns and the pock-marked relics of old colliery pits,
abandoned long ago. Fountains Fell gets its name from Fountains Abbey, but somehow it does not have the atmosphere of a
Christian place. It certainly carries the curses of many a lonely
walker and lacks the grace of Pen-y-ghent which, after crossing a
stone stile over a wall, now lies ahead. Before Pen-y-ghent there
is a sharp descent via a rocky path, which eventually bears right
at a wall **H** and leads straight down to a road. Turn left along the
road, cross a cattle grid, and head south-west past Rainscar.
Many of the field walls in this area are built from stones that

were first gathered by settlers in prehistoric times. Since then a hundred generations of farmers have set stone on stone, helping to create new pastures and meadows. Pen-y-ghent is very big now, and its stepped flanks look impossibly steep, but you will probably see people making their way uphill.

The Three Peaks of the Yorkshire Dales lie on a raised bed of Great Scar Limestone, the plateau on which limestone pavements have been weathered. Above this base rise cones or plinths of Yoredale rock, made up of bands of shale, sandstone and limestone. Uneven weathering of the Yoredales causes the characteristic stepped appearance of both Pen-y-ghent and Ingleborough (Whernside, the remainder of the trio, is rather more regular in shape). Pen-y-ghent has a very obvious broad band of limestone apparent halfway up its slope. The summits of all three of these mountains are capped by sandstone.

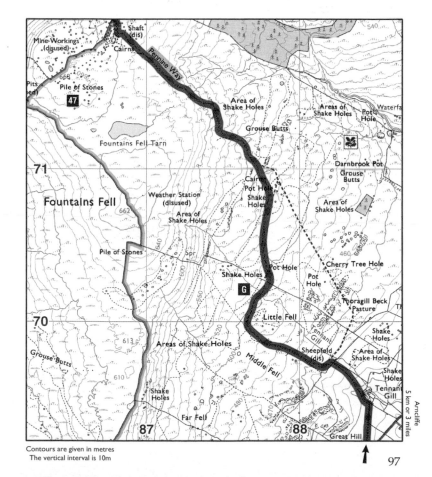

Contours are given in metres
The vertical interval is 10m

97

At Dalehead you turn right along a track (signed Pen-y-ghent) past a deep crater in the ground called Churn Milk Hole **48**. All the limestone country of the Great Scar is honey-combed by caves and the surface of the ground has shake-holes and sink-holes.

Just after Churn Milk Hole the track meets a T-junction, at which you turn right. This part of the route was so badly eroded that the National Park Authority spearheaded a major project to consolidate its surface. Sustainability is now the watchword.

After gaining height gradually, the Way crosses a ladder-stile and you face the southern edge of Pen-y-ghent **49**. There is no mistaking the path, which takes a direct line broken only by the obvious shelf of limestone. The two ascents on either side of the shelf are very steep but relatively short and have recently been pitched. You are soon at the summit cairn of Pen-y-ghent, which stands at 2,277 feet (694 metres). From the cairn and trig point you cross a ladder-stile over the wall that bisects Pen-y-ghent and goes north-east to Plover Hill.

Continuing along the route, you descend along a clear path and head north before turning sharp left **I** to begin a steeper descent on a surfaced path. Eventually the path levels and you bear right to meet a gate and stile. A network of paths radiates in all directions **J**; one leads over Horton Moor and another (heading north) to the impressive cavity called Hull Pot **50**, where the Hull Pot Beck disappears underground. You now go through a gate and head for civilisation, left down a very obvious green road, between parallel dry stone walls. A little way along this

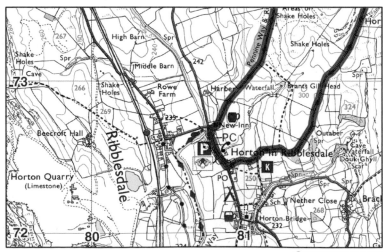

Contours are given in metres
The vertical interval is 10m

drove road is Tarn Bar **51**, a miniature version of Malham Cove, and beneath it a pretty, dry valley. Keep to the straight track, losing height gradually and passing attractive woodland plantations on the brow above Brackenbottom. The destination is never in doubt, but as the track begins to wind its way into Horton, bear right at a fork **K**, which brings you to the B6479 (Selside) road. From here turn right, to the bright lights of Horton in Ribblesdale.

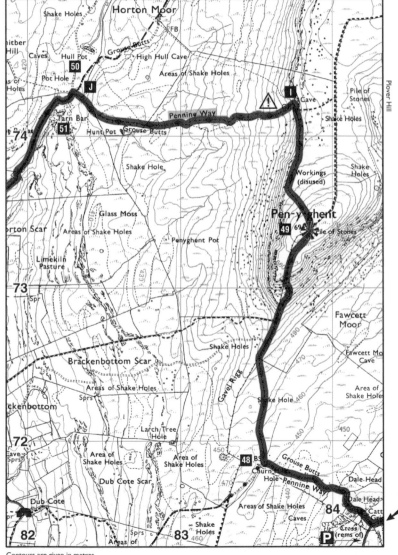

Contours are given in metres
The vertical interval is 10m

Scale approx 2¼ inches to 1 mile

Contours are given in metres
The vertical interval is 10m

CIRCULAR WALK: MALHAM

west walk: 5 miles (8 km)
east walk: 6 miles (9.7 km)

Malham is an ideal base for a weekend of walking in the Dales. The National Park car park south of the village provides a convenient starting point for several circular walks; two of these are marked on the map and use the Pennine Way as their central axis.

To start the west walk, head north up the Pennine Way past Town Head **40** to Malham Cove **41**. From the top of Malham Cove, where there is a limestone pavement **42**, bear north-west along the Watlowes valley **43**, then west and south-west over cropped limestone towards Kirkby Fell, before finally bearing south-east back into Malham and returning to the start.

100

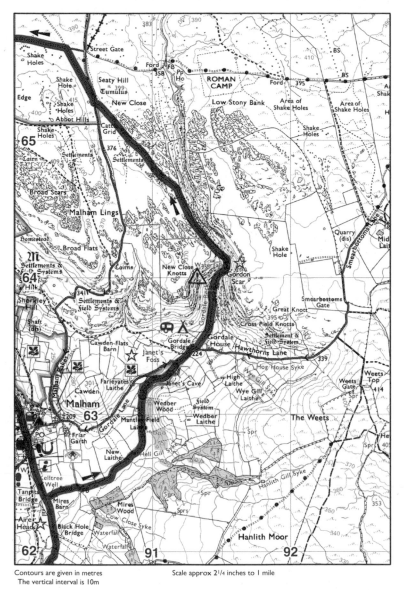

Contours are given in metres
The vertical interval is 10m

Scale approx 2¼ inches to 1 mile

For the east walk, head south along the Pennine Way, then turn left towards the waterfall of Janet's Foss. Follow Gordale Beck to Gordale Scar, taking care as you climb the steep slope. From here head north-west to Seaty Hill. Follow the road westwards, then turn left just south of Malham Tarn. At Comb Hill bear left to return along the Watlowes valley **43** to Malham Cove **41**, then walk back into Malham and the car park.

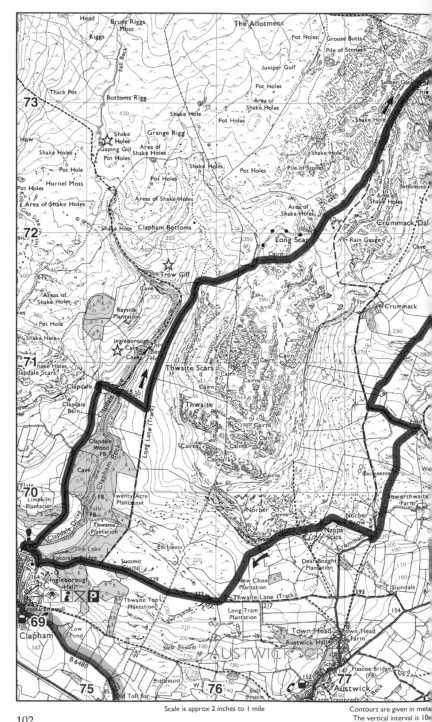

Scale is approx 2 inches to 1 mile

Contours are given in metre
The vertical interval is 10

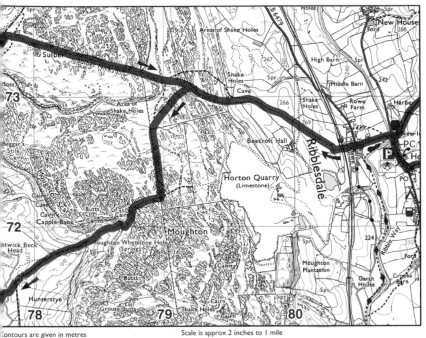

Contours are given in metres
The vertical interval is 10m

Scale is approx 2 inches to 1 mile

CIRCULAR WALK: HORTON IN RIBBLESDALE

11³/₄ miles (18.9 km)

One of the best starting points for a circular walk of the Ingleborough massif is Horton, from where a short climb westwards past the railway station and out of the village to the north of the massive Horton (or Beecroft) Quarry takes you uphill steadily. Where the path forks, bear south over a landscape of limestone pavement, then down to Norber with its famous group of erratics (ridges and boulders). The path meets Thwaite Lane and you then turn westward to the village of Clapham.

The return route begins along a stony track to Clapdale, but a more picturesque route is along the side of the lake, starting just before the turn on to the track, for which there is a small charge. These paths lead north towards Ingleborough cave. If you wish to see the cave and the dry valley of Trow Gill, head north but then return towards Clapdale and cross to the eastern side of the valley. Follow the valley north-eastwards until this meets a stony track and a clear footpath to Sulber. Once there you turn right, in the cleft between limestone pavement blocks called Sulber Nick, and continue south-south-east to meet the outward path back into Horton.

8 Horton in Ribblesdale to Hawes

over Cam Fell and Dodd Fell
13³/₄ miles (22.1 km)

The lonely valleys and bleak hills of Ribblehead contrast vividly with the Malham to Pen-y-ghent section of the Pennine Way. There are few outstanding landscape features, merely a gradual ascent out of Ribblesdale and a high-level trek over Cam Fell and Dodd Fell. There are very few farms or signs of civilisation, and although the route shadows the road you feel vulnerable, perhaps because of the wide views and the certain knowledge that you are on your own. When you walk into Hawes early, after a comparatively easy walk, you will wonder what all the fuss was about.

Heading north along the B6479 in Horton, past the café and car park, the Pennine Way follows the road across a bridge over a stream then, before the main bridge over the Ribble, turns right **A** in front of the Crown Inn (New Inn on the map). At the end of the inn car park, bear left up a very pretty walled green road lined with clover, lady's mantle and water avens. The views to left and right are of barns and meadows, the essence of the Dales, with the giants of Pen-y-ghent and Ingleborough above the shelves of Great Scar Limestone on either side of the dale.

Horton Church, on the roadside to the south of the village.

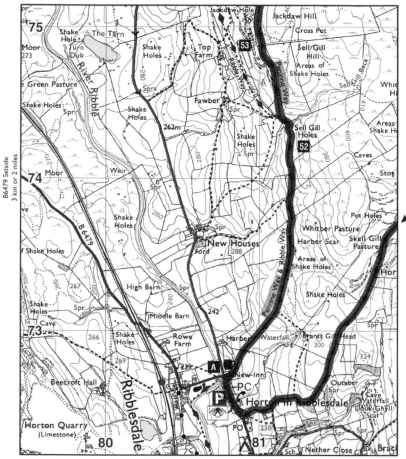

Contours are given in metres
The vertical interval is 10m

You gain height gradually, passing New Houses (and a new barn) in the valley to the left, then Sell Gill Holes **52**, a famous mecca for potholers. The cleft to the right of the track leads to a huge underground cavern, but only for those properly equipped. Through a gate, the Way continues with excellent views of limestone scars and terracettes, and some stretches of clints and grikes (ridges and clefts) **53** over the wall to the left.

Another cave entrance, Jackdaw Hole, is nearby. This is classic karst scenery. A glacier once flowed south, widening the valley and exposing shoulders of white limestone. When the ice retreated it left drumlins and erratics (ridges and boulders), and allowed the weather to work on the rock. The far flank of the valley contains some of the finest stretches of limestone pavement in the Dales. Much of this is grazed by sheep, but to the north-west at Colt Park (to the right of the little settlement of Selside) there is an enclosed ashwood, a national nature reserve where trees, ferns and rare alpine flowers flourish as they did in the interval between the retreat of the ice and the arrival of Stone Age farmers.

The Way follows the track along the rolling green road, usually beside a dry stone wall, with shake-holes and other suspicious grassy cavities in the moorland to the right. Eventually you cross a stream and go through a gate **B**, after which you leave the near wall behind. Another wall composed of pieces of limestone pavement can be seen to the right; the vegetation here is mainly moorland in character, but there are some 'lawns' of green grasses, close-cropped and with some familiar lowland flowers such as self-heal and marsh thistle. There are also some upland specialities to be found on these lime-rich flushes, most notably bird's-eye primrose.

Continue along the track and through another gate, but then turn left **C** away from the track, up over the hill brow with the edge of the extensive Greenfield conifer plantation to the right. Head down to a low saddle with Dismal Hill to the left, then bear left to follow the wall, on a track past the farm at Old Ing. Bear right before a gate, following a walled track (an old packhorse road) to another gate and stile. Over a wall to the right of this is a stream, which immediately disappears somewhere beneath your feet.

Continuing north, the Way contours around Cave Hill and Fair Bottom Hill and meets the deep limestone gorge of Ling Gill **54**. This is another national nature reserve, again dominated by ash trees but with rowan, aspen, birch and hazel in the understorey. It is possible that both Colt Park and Ling Gill are fragments of original sub-alpine forest, but they may result from regeneration after early efforts at farming had been abandoned. Rare plants, such as alpine cinquefoil, grow on the steep slopes, and even from the path it is possible to see patches of St John's wort, thyme, lady's bedstraw and wood cranesbill.

Through the gate the Way drops down to cross Ling Gill Bridge **55**, whose inscription, barely legible now, says 'ANNO 1765 THYS BRIDGE WAS REPAIRED AT THE CHARGE OF THE WHOLE OF WEST RYDEING'. After crossing the bridge, follow a track obliquely uphill, then wind north over peaty ground, rising all the time across open moorland, with hags to the right. Eventually the path meets a junction with another

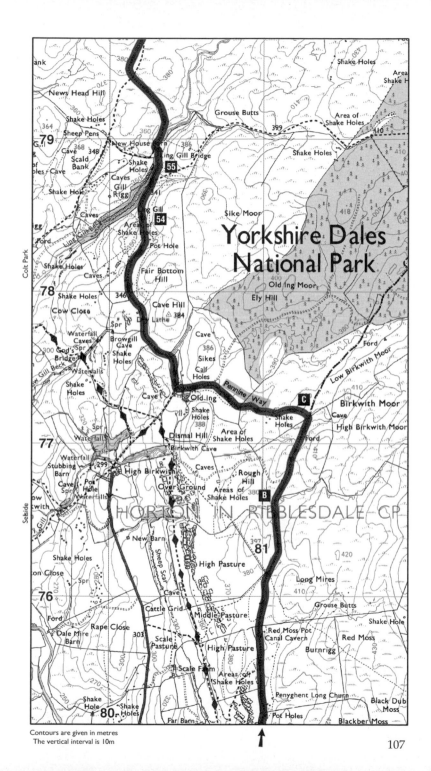

Contours are given in metres
The vertical interval is 10m

track **D**, the Dales Way. Turning right, the two trails coincide for a while over a well-worn thoroughfare across Cam Fell. Its origins may be prehistoric, but it was certainly used by the Romans and later by wool traders who called it Cam High Road. Even in dense mist the Pennine Way is easy to follow and the surface is good. Cam Houses **56** is the only settlement visible, but before this is reached there is a fork **E**, marked by a cairn, where the Pennine Way bears left to keep to the higher ground and the Roman road.

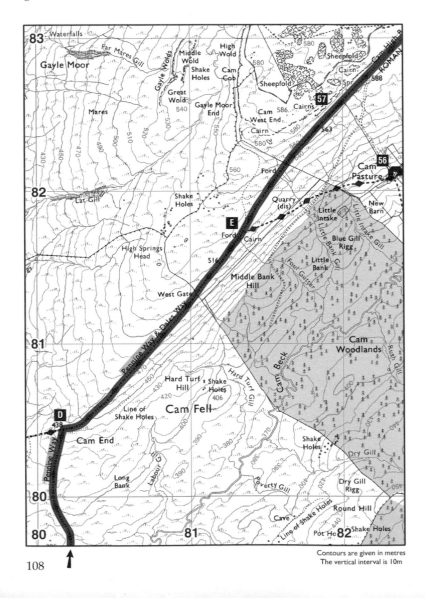

Contours are given in metres
The vertical interval is 10m

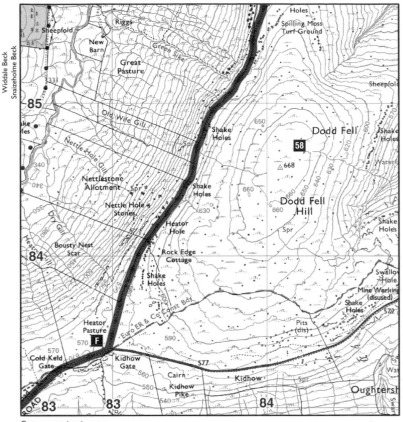

Contours are given in metres
The vertical interval is 10m

For a while you continue to climb (to about 1,840 feet/560 metres) but the route then levels off, with a valley to the right and a limestone edge **57** (hiding a block of pavement) to the left. When you meet a metalled road, follow it then bear left **F** on to a track (signed Hawes 5). This is the old packhorse route called West Cam Road. There is now a new valley on the left, steep-sided and with an arc of small streams ('gills' or 'sikes' depending on their size) that feed into Snaizeholme Beck, which joins Widdale Beck a little further down the valley.

To the right of the track is Dodd Fell **58**, which rises to 2,192 feet (668 metres). As you head north-east along an ancient track that seems to cling to the shoulder of the fell, it is clear that the classic limestone country has been left behind; bright green and dove grey have been replaced by the earth colours of ochre, sienna and olive. Surface water is more in evidence. The domed crest of Dodd Fell is covered with blanket bog. The route avoids it, rising to its highest point of the day – 1,870 feet (570 metres) – at Ten End **59**.

Late in the day this can seem a forsaken place, particularly if mist has closed in. However, from Ten End the whole atmosphere changes. Vistas open out to the east, across Sleddale to Wether Fell. Ahead is Wensleydale and its busy fretwork of dry stone walls and meadows. Beyond, directly to the north, lies Great Shunner Fell, with Buttertubs Pass and Lovely Seat to its right. The Way becomes a grassy path and you descend sharply along the crest of Rottenstone Hill. It follows a dry stone wall past Gaudy House, a pretty farmhouse (complete with spinning

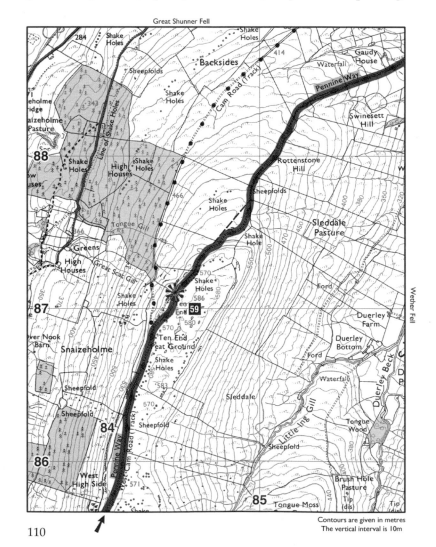

Contours are given in metres
The vertical interval is 10m

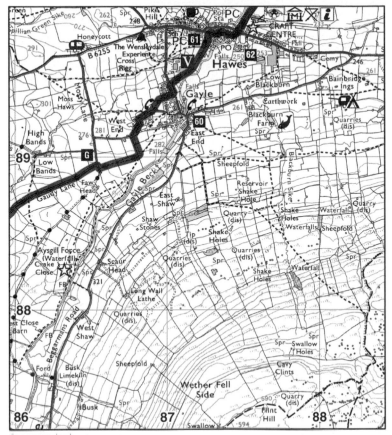

Contours are given in metres
The vertical interval is 10m

gallery) now renovated as holiday accommodation. Joining Gaudy Lane, a walled track between fields, the route continues to a road at which it turns right **G** then immediately left, through two hayfields, before turning downhill to the west end of the village of Gayle.

Civilisation is now close at hand. Cross the road, and go down the lane opposite, through the estate. This is the modern part of Gayle; its old bridge **60** is its most attractive feature, and is viewed by detouring into Gayle.

From the housing estate the Way turns left along a road, then right and along a pretty causey path of stone slabs above the Gayle Beck, with the old mill and bridge visible to the south. All that remains is to follow the path to the right of St Margaret's Church **61**, on to the main street of Hawes **62** opposite the White Hart Inn.

9 Hawes to Keld

over Great Shunner Fell and through Thwaite
12 ¹/₄ miles (19.7 km)

Hawes to Keld scores high on every walker's list: it is a beautiful, exhilarating and interesting section of the Pennine Way, beginning in the market town of Hawes in Wensleydale and crossing the River Ure to lead to Great Shunner Fell. From the top there is a long and easy descent into the meadowland of Swaledale, and from Thwaite another meadow and fell walk leads up Kisdon Hill and above the Swale to Keld.

Hawes **62** is the highest market town in Yorkshire and an important agricultural centre, with weekly sales of sheep and cattle at the auction mart. Until the 17th century, however, Hawes was smaller than its neighbour Gayle. The granting of a market charter in 1699 and the arrival of the turnpike road in 1795 led to rapid growth until eventually Hawes became the most important settlement in Upper Wharfedale. It is now home to the Dales Countryside Museum – well worth a visit.

From here the Pennine Way heads north, along the side road just west of the car park. Cross a bridge **A** over the disused railway line, then turn left off the road through a stile and across an area called Haylands. This is only a short cut to avoid the road-bend, but it offers an introduction to meadows, barns and a causey path. Back on the road, with sweet cicely growing along the verges, you cross the River Ure by the pretty Haylands Bridge **B** and follow the river for a while. Ahead, the road begins to climb, and above there is a flat-topped hill called Stags Fell, composed of Yoredale rocks with thick bands of sandstone. A line of old quarry workings shows how valuable this sandstone was in an area dominated by limestone, when every house and barn in the Dales had a slabbed roof. All the sandstone quarries are now closed.

You turn left **C** off the road along a footpath signed Pennine Way and Hardraw. The flat valley plain now lies to the left and you are soon following a causey-flagged route through meadows to Hardraw. You meet the road again at a single-arched bridge **63** across a stone-shelved beck. The centrepiece of Hardraw is a famous waterfall, Hardraw Force **64**, by which the beck tumbles down a wall of Yoredale rock just upstream from the Green Dragon Inn. The vertical fall of water is over 98 feet (30 metres). The waterfall can be reached along a private path from the Green Dragon, at which a small fee is charged.

Across the bridge, in the shade of cherry trees and horse chestnuts, past a tearoom, you leave Hardraw and turn right **D** off the road at a slate-sided house. The footpath is signposted Thwaite (Pennine Way) 8 and begins on a walled drove road, although you are soon on the open fell, where the mood begins to change. Buttercups give way to tormentil and swathes of mat-grass *Nardus stricta*, showing that the soil is no longer rich enough to support meadow grasses. Looking back, views begin to open out and Ingleborough becomes the clear skyline feature. The track is stony and quite steep; ignore other paths to the right and left. There are some limestone shelves with clumps of thyme, and during the summer the flowers attract the mountain bumblebee *Bombus monticola* and the small heath butterfly. Otherwise the vegetation is grazed by sheep and there are few flowers or insects.

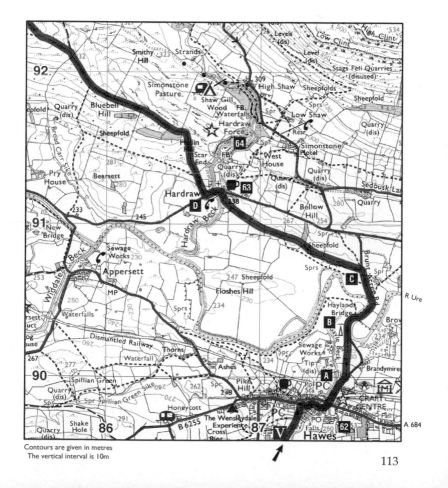

Contours are given in metres
The vertical interval is 10m

On the shoulder of the fell at Hearne Top there is a fork in the route **E**, where the Way takes the more northerly line and arcs right to keep with the main ridge. Fossdale Moss, across Hearne Beck in the east, becomes a dominant feature as the western views are obscured. At its head above Pickersett Edge stands a group of tall cairns that once overlooked a landscape of small coal pits and lead mines.

Apart from sheep, the only signs of life are upland birds: skylarks, pipits, wheatears, golden plovers and curlews. You continue onwards and upwards, brow to brow on a long climb past Crag End Beacon (a neat pile of stones) to breast another shoulder at Hearne Edge. Sections of the path are stone-slabbed, so you can enjoy a close look at the flora without getting wet. There are some good moorland plants here, partly because of the high altitude. This is also a likely spot to see dunlin. Less than 10,000 pairs of these wading birds nest in Britain, although they are common winter visitors. The dunlin likes high ground in summer, especially boggy moorland, so it is a Pennine speciality.

Hardraw Force, a short walk from the Green Dragon Inn.

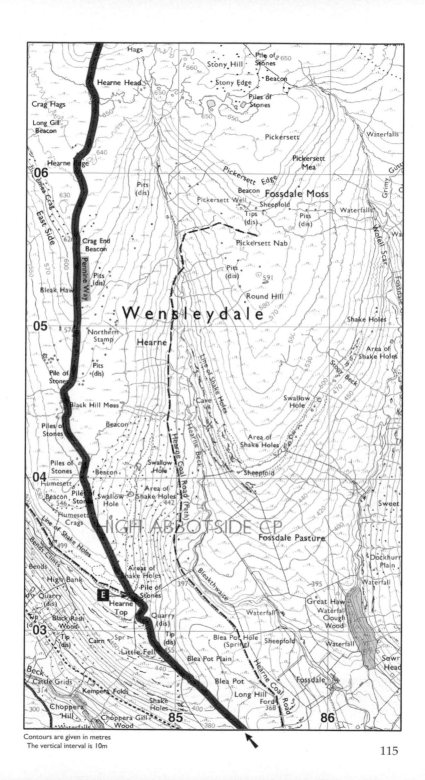

Contours are given in metres
The vertical interval is 10m

115

Great Shunner Fell, snow-flecked in the distance, is the main feature of the walk no...

...it of Hawes and Wensleydale.

At the summit of Great Shunner Fell **65** there is a post and wire fence along the crest close to the summit cairn, dulling any sense of wilderness. However, Great Shunner is high (2,350 feet/716 metres) and commands wonderful views. The weather is rarely benign, and the stone wind shelter gives little protection from bitter gales. From the summit cairn the route crosses a fence and heads north-east, dropping gradually to Beacon Cairn, then more sharply over marshy ground. There are now some long stone-slabbed sections of the route, and several of the steeper parts are pitched. To the left the views have completely changed; the valleys are Great Sled Dale and Birk Dale ('birk' is the old name for birch, suggesting that this area was once more extensively wooded). On the hill top is the cold, glassy pool of Birkdale Tarn. To the right is the valley of Thwaite Beck, leading into Swaledale.

The path arcs eastwards, above the gillheads and on stone slabs to avoid most of the peat flows. Eventually the path meets the top of a walled drove road **F** and enclosed fields appear on either side. Look back as you descend along the drove road: Great and Little Shunner stand side by side, and across the

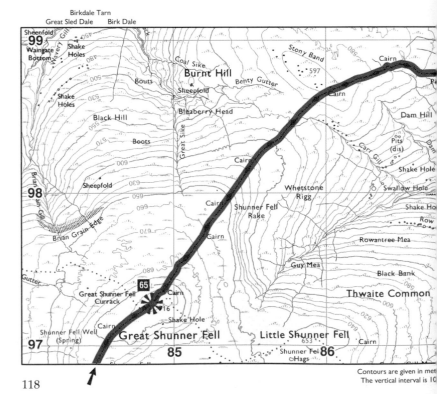

Contours are given in met
The vertical interval is 10

Thwaite and Cliff Becks, above Cliff Force and Lover Gill, rises Lovely Seat.

The route downhill towards Thwaite follows a narrow, stony track, and during midsummer it is much enlivened by beautiful meadows to left and right. The track meets a road at which you turn right **G**, past some sturdy field barns, and follow the road down into the village of Thwaite **66**. Below, to the right of the road, is Thwaite Beck **67**, which feeds peat-stained water to Straw Beck and the Swale. The 'dubs' (basins) in the shallow water always hold trout. Entering the village, the road passes an old chapel, converted into east and west flats, then the Kearton Restaurant – a sublime opportunity for a pot of tea that should not be dismissed lightly. The place is named after the Kearton brothers, Richard and Cherry, who spent their early years in Thwaite before moving to London. Both were famous in their day as naturalists, but Cherry Kearton was also a pioneer wildlife photographer. He made some ingenious hides, one of which was in the shape of a cow. A famous photograph shows this cow on its back with six feet in the air, the occupant having fainted after a long hot day in the field.

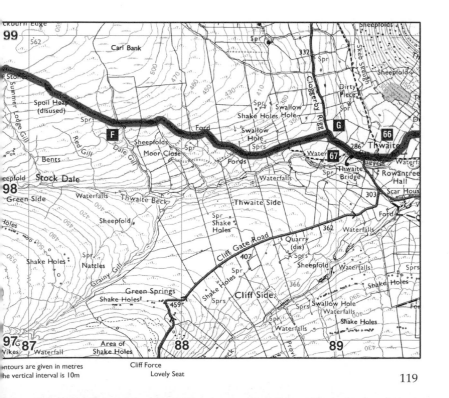

Cliff Force
Lovely Seat

Contours are given in metres
the vertical interval is 10m

From the narrow main street of Thwaite (the name, like the old village, is of Norse origin and means a clearing in the trees) the Pennine Way heads eastwards on a side street to a stile **H** beside a cottage, then follows a walled path and more stiles to bear left over meadowland, with Kisdon Hill rising steeply in the background. A sign (which we hope will endure) reminds everyone they are still in Yorkshire – 'NO CAMPING INT FIELD'. Dialect has its place, even on a prescriptive notice.

After crossing the lower meadows you begin to climb again, until 'inbye' fields (those located close to the farm) are left behind and the path is stony with patches of bilberry, cow wheat and thyme. The view back is excellent – of the village surrounded by a network of wobbly lined walls, and Great Shunner receding into the background. The Way takes a rather angular route around fields to a house, then left **I** up a walled track past a small kiln and around another field. The signing is good, the route clear, and there are now spectacular views eastwards across the upper Swale Valley to limestone scars and screes.

You head north along the shoulder of Kisdon Hill above the steep slope of North Gang Scar, then north-west following the contour of the valley. At Birk Hill the route drops below a cliff face where, among the scree and boulders, there are clumps of hart's-tongue fern, whitlow grass, pearlwort and shining cranesbill. Kisdon Force **68** lies immediately below, and the cleft in the opposite hillside carries the East Gill Beck **69** with its own little waterfall. The path is stony, sometimes over scree and therefore awkward, but route-finding is easy, through woodland and downhill to a meeting with the Coast-to-Coast Walk. Both routes cross the river at this point **J**. The village of Keld **70** lies a few hundred yards to the north.

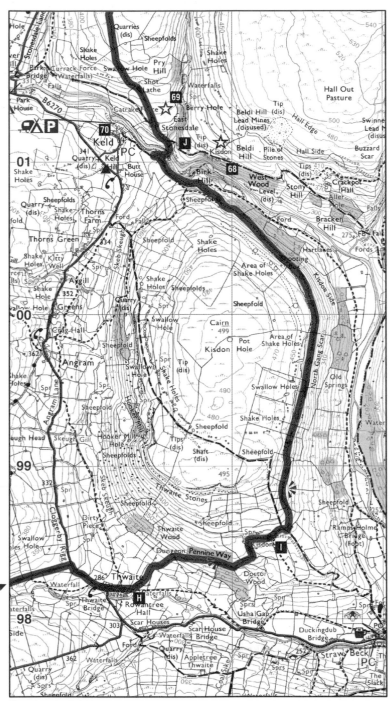

Contours are given in metres
The vertical interval is 10m

121

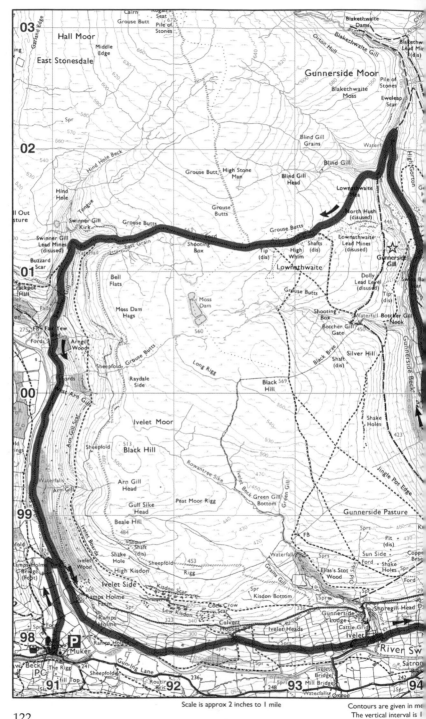

Scale is approx 2 inches to 1 mile

122

Contours are given in me
The vertical interval is 1

CIRCULAR WALK: SWALEDALE AND GUNNERSIDE

10 1/4 miles (16.5 km)

This walk from Muker does not start from the Pennine Way or use part of it, but it complements the Thwaite–Keld section and embraces all the classic elements of the Dales.

From the car park in Muker, follow a track north to cross the Swale by the Ramps Holme footbridge, then follow the Swale eastwards, across meadows to Gunnerside. Through the village and over a footbridge the route turns north along the east bank of Gunnerside Beck and Gunnerside Gill, past old lead mines and their associated 'hushes' (scoured valleys) to cross the stream at High Gorton. Climb steeply up the path to Lownathwaite, with more signs of lead mining, and head west over heather moorland to Swinner Gill where you descend to a limestone gorge, and cross Swinner Gill before heading south along the Swale again (the Pennine Way runs along the top of the steep slope on the opposite side of the river). The riverside path leads back to Ramps Holme footbridge and the start of the walk.

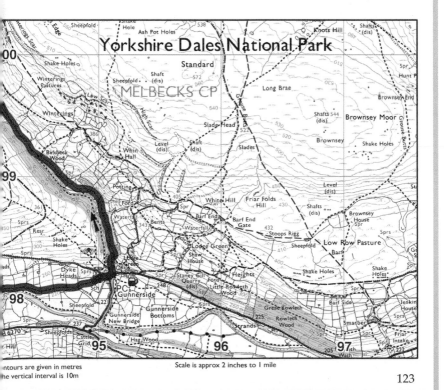

Contours are given in metres
The vertical interval is 10m

Scale is approx 2 inches to 1 mile

Meadows and barns

The hay harvest always marked a turning point in the farming year. A good crop of grass, cut, dried and stacked, meant a successful year. A wet harvest often spelt hardship. In the Yorkshire Dales the farmers reached a compromise with the weather, never expecting too much and being prepared to wait until high summer if necessary to take the cut. Each meadow had its own barn or byre, and sustained its own few head of cattle. During the summer these beasts grazed the 'outbye' pastures (those located away from the farm), but in the autumn they would be brought into the byre and the crop of hay, cut from the field and stored in the loft above the byre, would provide the necessary winter feed. The manure, of course, was spread over the field to keep the soil sweet and maintain its fertility.

This system of management took centuries to develop, but it has taken only a decade or two for it to become antiquated. Silage-making, the process of cutting grass earlier in the summer, then chopping it up and letting it pickle itself, has become accepted. By adding inorganic nitrogen fertilisers high yields are guaranteed, and the cutting and bagging can be carried out in almost any weather. However, the cost of increased quantity has been a sharp loss of quality. Old hay-meadows are full of flowers and have a great conservation value, because the crop is not cut until most of the seed has been set, so each year there is a full cycle of growth. By taking the cut much earlier, silage-making removes flowers before they have set seed, and the use of fertilisers increases the growth rate of high-yield grasses at the expense of other native grasses and flowers, which cannot compete.

There are not many meadows left in Britain, and the Yorkshire Dales are one of the few places where, because of their isolation, whole landscapes of flower-rich meadows and barns have survived. The recent designation of some of the Pennine Dales as an environmentally sensitive area and the work of the National Park Authority have encouraged farmers to 'go green'. In the future it may pay them to manage their meadows for the pleasure they give to visitors.

Meadow flowers grace the Dales for a very short time each year. The mix of species depends on the location, soil and climate, but many old meadows have 10 or 20 different species per square yard. Quaking grass, sweet vernal grass, meadow buttercup, bulbous buttercup, globeflower, eyebright, meadow saxifrage, wood cranesbill, dovesfoot cranesbill, ragged robin, common sorrel, red clover and northern marsh orchid are just a few of the flowers you may encounter in early summer.

Hay fields and barns are a particularly characteristic feature of Swaledale.

10 Keld to Bowes

via Tan Hill and Trough Heads
12¹/₂ miles (20.1 km)

Keld **70** is everyone's idea of a Dales village, small and hospitable, the last settlement to be found at the head of Swaledale. Above it lies Stonesdale, where a few meadows and barns provide a last glimpse of the classic Dales scenery before the Pennine Way climbs to the rugged moorland around Tan Hill, whose lonely inn lies in County Durham. To the north is the Stainmore Gap, which marks the end of this book and a convenient halfway point for the Way. Most people bound for Kirk Yetholm in one go turn north at Trough Heads to cross the River Greta at God's Bridge and make for an overnight stop (pre-booked) at

Kisdon Force, one of a series of waterfalls in Upper Swaledale.

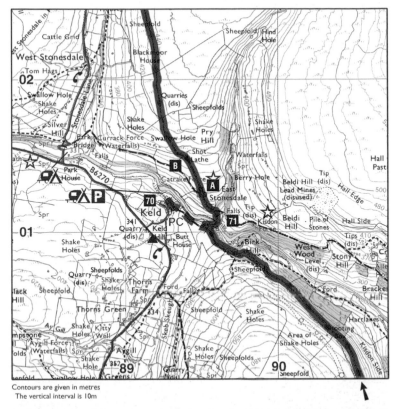

Contours are given in metres
The vertical interval is 10m

Baldersdale. (The route for this is described in National Trail Guide no. 6.) The alternative, and the logical stopping place if the route is being completed in sections, is to continue north-east at Trough Heads and make for the town of Bowes.

From Keld you backtrack along a south-easterly path, then head downhill on the Pennine Way to cross a bridge over the Swale and its wooded gorge. The route then passes East Gill Force **71**, an attractive little waterfall and one of a series marking a major geological fault.

Now you bear left on a steep track (a brief encounter with the popular Coast-to-Coast Walk) up to East Stonesdale Farm. Past the farmhouse the Way continues uphill along a grassy track **A** (not on the tarmac track, which marks the Coast-to-Coast route westwards). There are meadows on both sides as you progress along a walled drove road, but once past a gate and barn **B** both the meadows and the walls disappear, and you settle down to a long and gradual ascent through rough out-pasture.

The view back, of Kisdon Hill, is worth more than a passing glance. Ice shaped the landforms, but after the Ice Age the hill may have been an island, the site of Keld submerged beneath meltwater which then split to head south-east along the main Swaledale and south along the course of what is now the tiny Skeb Skeugh, to meet again at Muker. The cobwebbing of fields on the lower slopes and the ancient names for the settlements suggest that early farmers were quick to recognise the area's potential, although Swaledale was always isolated and for many centuries the villages were no more than clusters of houses.

You head north, on a shoulder of West Stonesdale with Birk Dale away to the left. There are a few meadows in the valley, but eventually these are left behind and the only signs of human endeavour are the side road across the valley and the grassed-over remains of lead mines and coal pits. After a

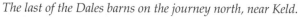
The last of the Dales barns on the journey north, near Keld.

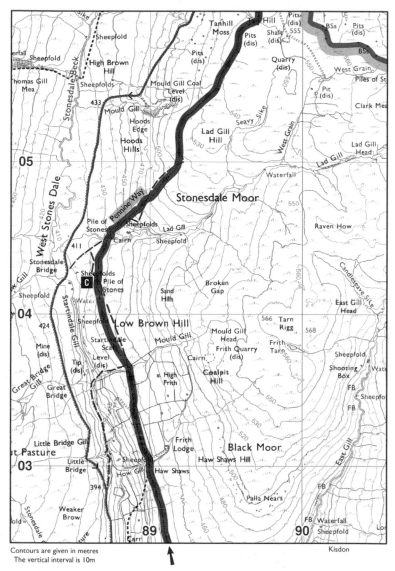

Contours are given in metres
The vertical interval is 10m

short walled section and a last barn by Mould Gill the route is
angled more steeply uphill and you bear right **C**, north-east,
following a groove in the hillside of Stonesdale Moor. The
track is now cairned and you follow an old packhorse trail
across a wild and remote stretch of moorland. To the east is
Lad Gill Hill and to the west the head of Stonesdale and
Drover Hole Sike. The track is closer to the side road by now,
and the two converge as they head north.

The isolated Tan Hill Inn **72** lies ahead. This area is pock-marked with colliery workings, mainly from the 19th century but with some nearly 600 years old. Tan Hill was also the meeting place for four packhorse trails.

The Way leads out to the Brough–Reeth road opposite the inn. After crossing the road you bear right, east of the inn, then left off the road again **D** before a cattle grid. You are now in County Durham and ahead lies Sleightholme Moor. In bad weather this can be a dangerous place, and you have an alternative route, following the road for 2 miles (3 km) before turning north-east at Great Cocker **E** to follow Sleightholme Moor Road (a track) and meet the Way beyond Hound Beck.

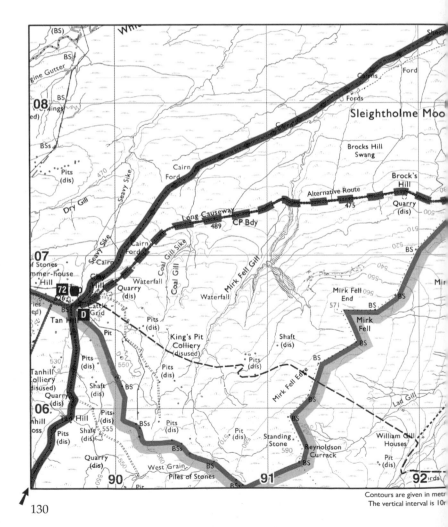

Contours are given in metr
The vertical interval is 10r

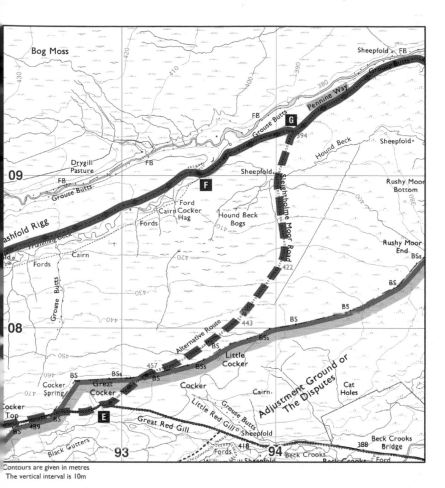

Contours are given in metres
The vertical interval is 10m

Heading north-east, below Clay Hill to the right, the road is visible up to Brock's Hill. This marks the division in catchment areas for two river systems, north-east into the Frumming Beck and, via Sleightholme Beck and the River Greta, into the Tees, or south-east into Black Gutters and, via Arkengarthdale and the Swale, into the Ouse. On such a wasteland of spongy peat the going is difficult and the route sometimes unclear, but it is straight and there are some cairns. Directly ahead in the far distance is Sleightholme farm. The Pennine Way stays on the left side of the Frumming Beck. Until recently the Pennine Way crossed the beck on to its south side, but you can now keep to the north side on more solid ground. Follow the new waymarked walk line, crossing three sleeper bridges before you meet a shooters' track at **F**. Eventually you meet a track **G** and continue along it past an L-shaped sheep-shelter and on to a metalled track leading to Sleightholme farm. After the farm and past a barn, the Way turns off the road, then left through a gate and across open pasture and meadowland down towards a bridge.

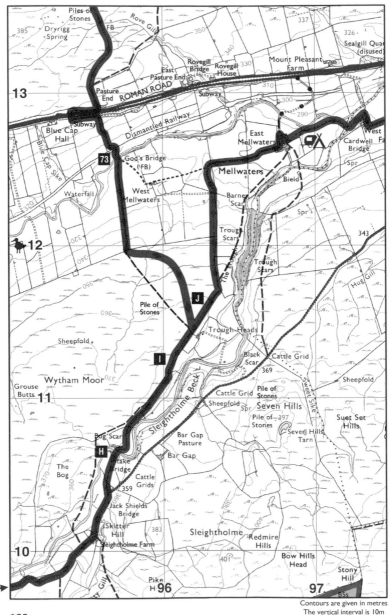

Contours are given in metres
The vertical interval is 10m

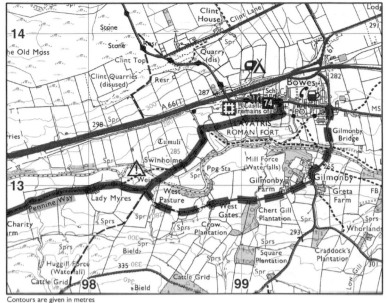

Contours are given in metres
The vertical interval is 10m

Across Intake Bridge **H** a path leads uphill to follow a route parallel with Sleightholme Beck towards Trough Heads. Bear left through a gate **I** on to the moor and continue beside the wall to **J** where the route splits. If you are continuing to Baldersdale, turn left and head north then west across heather moorland to a bridlegate. Go through the gate, after which the Way is clear down to the River Greta at God's Bridge **73**, where the river disappears beneath a great slab of limestone. On the north side of the Greta you pass an old lime kiln, through a disused railway embankment, and climb a track towards the A66, where the route has been diverted via an underpass beneath the busy trunk road. The next section of the route, over Cotherstone Moor to Baldersdale, appears in National Trail Guide no. 6.

To take the 'Bowes Loop' from Trough Heads the route continues north-east, following a wall as it bears north downhill (that is, not following the river). You meet a track at which the route turns right to East Mellwaters farm, then left to circle the farm before turning left in the yard past cow sheds; you now continue close to the river and to the left of a wall, crossing Cardwell Bridge (over Sleightholme Beck again) and circling West Charity Farm. The square, 12th-century Bowes Castle **74** dominates the view ahead. The pastoral elegance of Bowes contrasts sharply with the windswept mires to north and south.

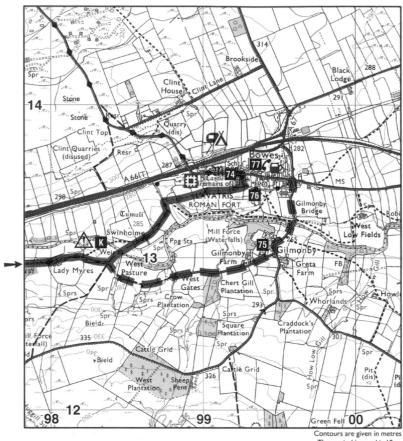

Contours are given in metres
The vertical interval is 10m

Through Lady Myres farm, but before the next farm at West Pasture, you turn left off the track and head down to the river bank. Cross using stepping stones near the weir **K**, but be careful. A footbridge would make crossing easier. If the river is in spate the alternative is to go back to the track and continue along to Gilmonby **75** and cross the bridge there. If the river is fordable (and it usually is), cross it and climb the path up the far bank to Swinholme. A metalled track then veers north, but halfway along you turn right over a wooden fence and head east across the hollow of a field to a gate, then over more fields via stiles, to cut across the grass-covered remains of the Roman fort of Lavatrae **76**. A slight detour after the gates will take you around the ruins of Bowes Castle **74** (details are included in National Trail Guide no. 6) before continuing along a narrow side road on to the main street of Bowes **77**.

On Sleightholme Moor the Way keeps company with Frumming Beck and Sleightholme Beck.

PART THREE

USEFUL
INFORMATION

Many of the characteristics that make the Pennine Way such an exciting prospect – the remote terrain, lack of roads and absence of towns – make it extremely difficult to plan a walk, because public transport and accommodation are limited. The following notes are intended as a précis of planning information, referring to more comprehensive services where these are available. Details of transport and accommodation, which will be necessary for planning, are included for the whole of the Pennine Way, north and south. These are followed by details of useful regional addresses and a bibliography of titles of use on the southern half of the Way.

All Pennine Way walkers should be aware of the Pennine Way Association, which exists to protect the Way and to provide information and a forum in which organisations and individuals can get together to discuss matters relating to the Way. Details about associate membership can be obtained from the Secretary: Peter Stott, 3 Bower Drive, Crich, Matlock, Derbyshire, DE4 5NF.

Transport

The principal public transport points along the Way are as follows (adapted from the Pennine Way Association booklet):

Edale: some trains to and from Manchester and Sheffield stop at Edale. Tel. (0161) 832 8353, the main enquiry office in Manchester.

Standedge: bus services between Huddersfield and Oldham extend to Manchester on Saturday, passing the door of Globe Farm.

Hebden Bridge: the Liverpool–Manchester–Leeds line passes through Hebden Bridge frequently during the week and also has a Sunday service. Tel. (0161) 832 8353.

Haworth: the private Worth Valley line stops at Haworth. This takes you to the main station at Keighley, to connect with BR. Tel. (01535) 645214 for train times.

Thornton-in-Craven: a Pennine Motors coach (tel. (01756) 749215) runs between Colne, Earby and Skipton, calling at Thornton-in-Craven. Trains from Colne and Skipton run to Leeds and Manchester.

Gargrave: Pennine Motors runs a service to Gargrave; from here there are buses to Skipton, Settle and Malham. Tel. (01756) 749215.

Malham: tel. (01756) 749215 for buses to Skipton via Gargrave.

Horton in Ribblesdale: trains run north to Carlisle and south to Leeds.

Hawes: a bus goes from here to Richmond. You can get a further bus to connect with BR at Darlington. For services from Hawes to Garsdale, contact Hawes National Park Centre, tel. (01969) 667450.

Thwaite and Keld: a bus service is run to Richmond Monday–Friday by Arriva North East Tel. (01642) 67225.

Middleton in Teesdale has an infrequent bus service to Darlington. Tel. Arriva North East (01642) 67225 for the times.

Dufton: the nearest public transport is at Appleby where there is a station on the Leeds–Settle–Carlisle line.

Alston: Wright Brothers runs coaches from Alston to Haltwhistle via Slaggyford. Tel. (01434) 381200.

Twice Brewed: the Carlisle–Newcastle bus stops here hourly. Tel. (01228) 819090 for details.

Hadrian's Wall: a bus service runs daily between Hexham and the main Wall sites during July and August. Tel. Northumberland National Park on (01434) 605555.

Bellingham: Tyne Valley Coaches runs a service to Hexham for BR connection to Newcastle. Tel. (01434) 602217.

Byrness: a National Express service runs daily from Newcastle to Edinburgh. Tel. 08705 808080.

Kirk Yetholm: Munro's of Jedburgh run a daily service to Kelso. Tel. (01835) 862253. Another service runs from Kelso to Jedburgh, where connections can be made with Newcastle and Edinburgh.

Accommodation

The Pennine Way Association produces an invaluable *Accommodation and Camping Guide* with up-to-date lists of addresses. This costs £1.50 (plus an A5 s.a.e.) and is obtainable from John Needham, 23 Woodland Crescent, Hilton Park, Prestwich, Manchester, M25 8WQ.

The Youth Hostels Association operate a Booking Bureau for youth hostels along the Pennine Way. Contact: YHA Booking Bureau, PO Box 6028, Matlock, Derbyshire, DE4 3XB. Tel. 0870 770 6113. Fax. (01629) 592627.

Members of the Ramblers' Association (address on page 142) will find some accommodation information in their yearbook. Otherwise, the best way to book overnight bed and breakfast is through tourist information centres or National Park centres. These will also have up-to-date lists of camp sites. The Yorkshire Dales National Park also produces its own accommodation guide.

Tourist information centres (TICs) are also a useful source of local information. The following are the TICs in the vicinity of the Pennine Way:

Edale National Park Visitor Centre (a Peak National Park Centre), Fieldhead, Edale, Hope Valley, S33 7ZA. Tel. (01433) 670207.

Glossop TIC, The Gatehouse, Victoria Street, Glossop, Derbyshire, SK13 8HT. Tel. (01457) 855920.

Hebden Bridge TIC, Bridge Gate, Hebden Bridge, West Yorkshire, HX7 8JP. Tel. (01422) 843831.

Haworth TIC, 2/4 West Lane, Haworth, West Yorkshire, BD22 8EF. Tel. (01535) 642329.

Skipton TIC, 35 Coach Street, Skipton, North Yorkshire, BD23 1LG. (01756) 792809.

Settle TIC, Town Hall, Cheapside, Settle, North Yorkshire, BD24 9EJ. Tel. (01729) 825192.

Horton in Ribblesdale Tourist Information Point, Pen-y-Ghent Café, Horton in Ribblesdale, North Yorkshire, BD24 0HE. Tel. (01729) 860333.

National Park Centre, Station Yard, Hawes, North Yorkshire, DL8 3NT. Tel. (01969) 667450.

Middleton in Teesdale TIC, 10 Market Place, Middleton in Teesdale, County Durham, DL12 0QG. Tel. (01833) 641001.

Brough TIC, The 'One Stop' Shop, Main Street, Brough, Cumbria, CA17 4BL. Tel. (01768) 341260.

Appleby-in-Westmorland TIC, The Moot Hall, Boroughgate, Appleby-in-Westmorland, Cumbria, CA16 6XE. Tel. (01768) 351177.

Alston TIC, The Town Hall, Front Street, Alston, Cumbria, CA9 3RF. Tel. (01434) 382244.

Haltwhistle TIC, The Railway Station, Station Road, Haltwhistle, Northumbria, NE49 9HN. Tel. (01434) 322002.

Once Brewed Visitor Centre, Military Road, Bardon Mill, Hexham, Northumbria, NE47 7AN. Tel. (01434) 344396.

Hexham TIC, Wentworth Car Park, Hexham, Northumbria, NE46 1QE. Tel. (01434) 652220.

Kelso TIC, The Town House, The Square, Kelso, Borders, TD5 7HF. Tel. 0870 608 0404.

The principal overnight stopping places on the Way are:

Edale (YH; b & b; camping)
Crowden (YH; camping)
Globe Farm, Standedge (b & b; camping)
Mankinholes (YH)
Ponden (b&b; camping)
Earby (YH)
Lothersdale (b & b; camping)
Malham (YH; b & b; camping; bunkhouse barn)
Horton-in-Ribblesdale (b & b; camping)
Hawes (YH; b & b; camping)
Keld (YH; b & b)
Bowes (b & b; camping)
Baldersdale (YH; limited b & b; camping)
Holwick (camping; bunkhouse barn)
Langdon Beck (YH; b & b)
Dufton (YH; b & b; camping)
Garrigill (b & b; camping; bunkhouse barn)
Alston (YH; b & b; camping)
Greenhead (YH; b & b; camping)
Once Brewed (YH; b & b; camping)
Bellingham (YH; b & b; camping)
Byrness (YH; b & b)
Coquetdale and Uswayford (limited b & b)
Kirk Yetholm (YH; b & b; camping)

Useful addresses

Countryside Agency (Headquarters), John Dower House, Crescent Place, Cheltenham, Gloucestershire, GL50 3RA. Tel. (01242) 521381.

Countryside Agency, North-West Regional Office, 7th Floor, Bridgwater House, Whitworth Street, Manchester, M1 6LT. Tel. (0161) 237 1061.

Countryside Agency, Yorkshire and Humberside Regional Office, 4th Floor, Victoria Wharf Embankment IV, Sovereign Street, Leeds LS1 4BA. Tel. (0113) 246 9222.

English Nature, North-East England Regional Sub-Office, Asquith House, Leyburn Business Park, Harmby Road, Leyburn, North Yorkshire, DL8 5QA. Tel. (01969) 623447.

English Nature, West Midlands Region, Manor Barn, Over Haddon, Bakewell, Derbyshire, DE45 1JE. Tel. (01629) 815095.

National Trust, East Midlands Regional Office, Clumber Park Stableyard, Worksop, Nottinghamshire, S80 3BE. Tel. (01909) 486411.

Ordnance Survey, Romsey Road, Maybush, Southampton, SO16 4GU. Tel. 08456 050505.

Peak National Park Office, Aldern House, Baslow Road, Bakewell, Derbyshire, DE45 1AE. Tel. (01629) 816200.

Pennine Way Association, Peter Stott, Secretary, 3 Bower Drive, Crich, Matlock, Derbyshire, DE4 5NF.

Ramblers' Association, 2nd Floor, Camelford House, 87–90 Albert Embankment, London, SE1 7TW. Tel. (020) 7339 8500.

Yorkshire and Humberside Tourist Board, 312 Tadcaster Road, York, YO2 2HF. Tel. (01904) 707961.

Yorkshire Dales National Park, Colvend, Hebden Road, Grassington, Skipton, North Yorkshire, BD23 5LB. Tel. (01756) 752748.

Yorkshire Wildlife Trust, 10 Toft Green, York, YO1 6JT. Tel. (01904) 659570.

Youth Hostels Association, Trevelyan House, Dimple Road, Matlock, Derbyshire, DE4 3YH. Tel. 0870 770 8868.

Bibliography

Over the years there have been several excellent books about the Pennine Way, though not as many as might be expected. Some of the most interesting are now long out of print, such as J.D. Wood's delightful *Mountain Trail* (published by Allen & Unwin in 1947). The following is a list of standard Pennine Way titles, together with books describing other aspects relating to the southern half of the route.

Anderson, P. and Shimwell, D., *Wild Flowers and other Plants of the Peak District* (Moorland, 1981).

Ford, Trevor D. and Rieuwert, J. H. (ed.), *Lead Mining in the Peak District* (Peak Park Joint Planning Board, 1983).

Forder, John and Forder, Eliza, *Hill Shepherd* (Frank Peters, 1989).

—— and Raistrick, Arthur, *Open Fell, Hidden Dale* (Frank Peters, 1985).

Hardy, G., *North to South along the Pennine Way* (Frederick Warne, 1983).

Hartley, Mary and Ingibly, Joan, *Life and Tradition in the Yorkshire Dales* (J. M. Dent, 1968).

Peel, J. H. B., *Along the Pennine Way* (David & Charles, 1972).

Pilton, B., *One Man and his Bog* (Corgi, 1986).

Raistrick, Arthur, *The Pennine Dales* (Eyre Methuen, 1968).

—— *Malham and Malham Moor* (Dalesman, 1983).

Smith, Roland, *The Peak National Park* (Webb & Bower / Michael Joseph, 1987).

—— *First and Last, the Peak National Park in words and pictures* (Peak Park Joint Planning Board, 1989).

Waltham, Tony, *Yorkshire Dales: Limestone Country* (Constable, 1987).

—— *Yorkshire Dales National Park* (Webb & Bower / Michael Joseph, 1987).

Wainwright, A., *Pennine Way Companion* (Michael Joseph, 1968).

—— *Wainwright on the Pennine Way* (Michael Joseph, 1985).

Wright, C. J., *A Guide to the Pennine Way* (Constable, 1987, 4th edition).

Wright, Geoffrey, *Roads and Trackways of the Yorkshire Dales*, (Moorland, 1985).

—— *The Yorkshire Dales* (David & Charles, 1987).

The Peak National Park, Yorkshire Dales National Park (addresses on page 142) and Calderdale Leisure Services Department of the Metropolitan Borough of Calderdale all produce good walks leaflets and other useful material. These may be obtained either by writing to the National Parks involved or by calling in at a visitor centre or tourist information centre. Information about Calderdale is best obtained from the Hebden Bridge Tourist Information Centre (see page 140).

Ordnance Survey Maps covering the Pennine Way (South)

Landranger Maps: 92, 98, 103, 109, 110
Explorer Maps: OL1, The Peak District (Dark Peak area);
    OL2, Yorkshire Dales; OL21, South Pennines;
    OL30, Yorkshire Dales (Northern & Central areas).
Motoring Maps: Reach the Pennine Way (South) using
    Routemaster Map 5, 'Northern England'.

Further Information

For the latest information on the Pennine Way National Trail visit the official website: www.nationaltrail.co.uk. The website provides a one-stop shop for all the information needed to prepare for the walk, from route map to accommodation guide. It is also packed full of stunning photography of the 268-mile National Trail.

You can also order a useful pack of leaflets that provide details on the Trail, accommodation and public transport from:

The Pennine Way National Trail Officer
The Countryside Agency
4th Floor, Victoria Wharf
4 The Embankment
Sovereign Street
Leeds LS1 4BA
Tel. (0113) 246 9222
E-mail: pennineway@countryside.gov.uk